HOW TO ANALYZE PEOPLE: THE ULTIMATE GUIDE TO SPEED READING, BODY LANGUAGE, AND BEHAVIORAL PSYCHOLOGY USE OTHER PEOPLE'S BODY SIGNALS TO UNDERSTAND THE CHARACTER USING EMOTIONAL INTELLIGENCE

Learn To Analyze People, Easy Understand Body Language And Personality Types, Reading People And Human Psychology

of explanation, in this book, the proprietors are not partnered with the trademarks and brand.

4

TABLE OF CONTENTS

HOW TO ANALYZE PEOPLE 5

INTRODUCTION 6

MODELS TO UNDERSTAND HUMAN BEHAVIOR 9

PERSONALITY 17

DO START WITH PEOPLES YOU KNOW 41

THE ART OF EFFECTIVE QUESTIONING 53

STEP BY STEP INSTRUCTIONS TO READ PEOPLE LIKE A PRO: 16 TRICKS FROM PSYCHOLOGY 74

DISCOVERING PATTERNS 85

LEARNING THE ART AND SECRETS OF NONVERBAL COMMUNICATION.. 102

NEGATIVE BODY LANGUAGE: EXAMPLES AND SIGNS...................... 135

POSITIVE BODY LANGUAGE: EXAMPLES AND SIGNS 141

SIMPLE UNDERSTAND BODY LANGUAGE 152

BODY AND FACIAL EXPRESSIONS... 161

HOW TO ANALYZE PEOPLE

INTRODUCTION

If you look at someone and feel like you can judge whether they're in a good mood or a bad mood, whether they're a nice person or a mean person or anything else at all, you're reading them. In general, reading someone means looking at them (and it doesn't just have to be a cursory glance) and knowing something about them without saying anything at all. It's a feeling that you get from looking at them and observing the way they stand, the way they look around, the way they move. Several different features could play into your opinion and understanding of them, but the most important thing is that they haven't explicitly told you anything.

Now, a lot of people take a cursory look at someone and believe they know something. You think to yourself,' oh, they look friendly' or' they look upset.' These are instinctual opinions and thoughts that we have as soon as we see a person. As we begin to talk to them, we may come to new conclusions, or even as we look across the room. You never may speak to him, but you have thoughts and thoughts about the kind of person you saw. You read them, and whether you're right or wrong is a secondary point.

WHY IS IT IMPORTANT TO READ PEOPLE?

Why would you even bother reading people? Well, there are several different reasons why this can be a useful skill. First, at the most basic level, it lets you know how to approach someone. If they look friendly, you might be more willing to come up with a smile and a warm greeting. If they seem unhappy, you might be more likely to come up with a reason than stop and say hello. If a friend appears angry, you might ask them what's going on or what's going on. Understanding what they're feeling from a glance can help you anticipate what's going on just like that, and the better you get with the skill, the better you're talking to people.

If you don't know how to read people at all, you might end up interpreting something that they do or an action or a facial expression incorrectly, and you might start assuming things about a person that isn't accurate. You might see their face and think they're an angry person when they're just upset about a situation. You may think they look unfriendly, but they're just frustrated with something that's going on around them. By learning to read better, you're going to be able to advance your life in many ways.

Reading people can help you understand who you can approach this great new idea (and when) and from whom you should be clear. It also lets you know how to introduce something to them, whether from a factual point of view or more fun and creative. Before you know it, reading people is going to be second nature to you if you practice it often enough. And what's even better is that you've probably been doing it all your life, not even thinking about it. That's because it's something that even kids will try out from time to time, without knowing how important it is. Reading People In Childhood When you were a kid, did you ever sit on a bench in the park or on your porch and watch people walk around? You probably did that at some point, even if it was just a couple of minutes. And then you're going to look at the people and make stories. If they walk a dog, they might be a dog walker on their way to the park. If they're carrying a briefcase and walking fast, they're late for a big meeting (that may have been a meeting with aliens in your young mind, of course, but you get a general idea).

You've already interpreted what you see from someone to make a story about them.

As you get older, you use the same kinds of skills to start reading people even more (and a little more precisely). Your understanding of facial expressions and postures begins to develop a little more, and before you know it, you can look at someone and immediately know what they're feeling (at least most of the time). All it takes is a little bit of cultivation for your childhood skills, and before you know it, you're on the path to greater success in your adult life.

MODELS TO UNDERSTAND HUMAN BEHAVIOR

Early old-style approaches made the presumptions that people are generally languid and self-serving, unbiased, or positive and self-motivated. In more straightforward terms, they should be pushed and controlled and held under observation, never to be trusted to place in a great day's worth of effort without anyone else.

It took into account only monetary prizes. Close and compelling monitoring has also suggested.

Frameworks and possibility scholars saw people as versatile and felt that quite a bit of behavior was found out and not owing to inclinations to be negative or positive.

The discoveries of human relations scholars Likert, McGregor, and Bennis, had a positive perspective on human nature. They have been creating and spreading them. Representatives supported personal and social success. Whenever left alone, they would buckle down for the inborn fulfillment of occupation all around done-The accentuation was on popularity based choice making and administration. Rules were to be testing and permitted the personalrepresentative to be imaginative.

Models of Human Behavior

Psychoanalytic Model: Freudian methodology relies upon the strife model of humans. By utilizing clinical systems of free affiliation and psychotherapy, Freud felt that behavior isn't in every case, intentionally clarified. "Oblivious" is the primary consideration that manages the person's behavior.

Person's behavior relies upon **three components:**

(I) ID, (ii) Ego (iii) Super sense of self.

ID:

By ID, it implies delight. To a certain level of having an ID in an individual is valuable yet may likewise prompt ruinous propensities like being forceful, overwhelming, battling, and for the most part, obliterated. This intuitive is more ruling in childhood. Be that as it may, when people create and develop, they figure out how to control the ID. Be that as it may, it is continuously oblivious. All through life, the 'ID' becomes a significant wellspring of reasoning and carrying on.

SELF IMAGE:

Ego speaks to 'cognizant' arrange in one's behavior. Even though Id comes in strife with a sense of self, the conscience relies upon the super personality.

SUPEREGO:

It speaks to "still, small voice." An individual doesn't know about the superego's working. The still small voice is reliant on two factors that are social qualities and lessonsof the general public. Superego's improvement generally depends on the parent's impact.

When the youngster grows up, the kid will unwittingly relate to guardians esteem, furthermore, ethics.

There is consistently tussle between the id, sense of self, and superego.Each level of the individual varies by person — This model supports the different behaviors of an adult.

In any case, the cutting edge speculations have seriously scrutinized this hypothesis as it did not depend on any experimental certainties, and thus, it can not be acknowledged in totality. However, the idea of "oblivious" is a massive commitment to understanding the explicit behavior of humans.

Existential Model: This model isn't experimentally based. Its base is writing andreasoning.

Existentialists recognize that this condition's depersonalizing effects allow people to make their destiny. Thus, people shape their character. Moreover, their "reality" is essential and beneficial.

The urbanization currently occurred is even more evident. Because people are so greedy and busy, they do not have energy with conventional qualities and standards, and it sometimes becomes illogical to tackle them. The existential model is particularly apparent when used today.

While this model does not make sense, it certainly can be used to understand human behavior.

Internal versus External Determinants of Behavior

Condition assumes a significant job in molding behavior, and innate gift and character advancement are affected by our authentic legacy.

Character versus the Environment

Personality and situational factors must be taken into account, to clarify conduct, although an accent on earth will be essential or perhaps rather important rather than an emphasis on character qualities.

Insight versus the Environment

To comprehend one's behavior, we shouldknow the person's past reactions to comparable (upgrade) circumstances and the prizes or disciplines that pursued that reaction.

There are two models, which leave these methodologies:

Behavioristic Model: In this model, the behavior is subject to two components, i.e., upgraded and reaction. Learning happens with this sort of model. Pavlov and

Watson, with their examination, felt that behavior could be best understood byimprovement and response.

Behaviorist model is said to be SR (Stimulus-Response)

Intellectual Model: S-OR-R. This model underlines the positive and unrestrained choice components of human creatures and utilizes ideas, for example, hope, request, and motivation.

Tolman, with his investigations, found that the premise of learning as of 'anticipation' which is comprehended as one specific occasion prompting a particular result, i.e., objective. Human behavior depends on these objectives.

The subjective model is said to be:

S - O - R (Stimulus-Organism-Response model)

The two methodologies consider figuring out how to be nature as majorly affecting behavior.

From these various methodologies, it very well may be said that:

Behavior is brought about by impulses, hereditary foundation, and character qualities that are developed at an early age. Change is extremely hard for the individual, and that one's ability is severely constrained.

Behavior is, for the most part, learned through our connections with nature.

Present occasions, as opposed to past incidents, are significant. Even though there are few confinements on one's abilities, one is fit for incredible measures of progress.

Suggestions For The Organization

The behavior of people is caused, and pursues an example; along these lines, the action isunusual. The investigation of behavior is nevertheless, fulfilling and fundamental for the board. It is suspicious whether the supervisor can play out his undertakings acceptably without building up a reasonable level of comprehension of the people around him.

Any endeavor to realize why people carry on as they do in associations requires a few comprehensions of individual contrasts. Administrators invest significant energy in making decisions about the fit between people, work errands, and from these methodologies, there is presumably a fantastic agreement that the Earth has a far more significant effect than is accepted.

The suggestions for the associations are substantial. It implies that large regions of human behavior are modifiable.

Hierarchical plans, preparing, and advancement can profoundly affect the behavior of individuals from an association.

PERSONALITY

Gordon Allport characterized Personality as the dynamic association inside the individual of those Psycho-Physical Systems that decide his one of a kind acclimations to his condition.

Personality can be portrayed all the more explicitly as "how an individual influences others, how he comprehends and sees himself and his example of inward and external quantifiable traits."

From this definition, it tends to be comprehended one's physical appearance and behavior influences others. Understanding oneself methods one is one of a kind with a lot of frames of mind and values and a self-idea. At long last, the example of quantifiable traits alludes to a lot of attributes that the individual displays.

A portion of different definitions are "Personality is a vehicle to incorporate recognition, learning, qualities, and frames of mind and accordingly to comprehend the complete individual."

Personality isan individual's all out feeling of self; it is an arranging power for the people specific example of showed traits and behaviors." "Personality is the perfection of encounters and hereditary impacts." Personality is affected by individual life and where he is working.

DETERMINANTS OF PERSONALITY

Personality is the consequence of both heredity, condition, and circumstance.

HEREDITY

Heredity alludes to those elements that were Set aside at origination. Physical appearance, personality, vitality level, and organic rhythms are the qualities which are by and significantly impacted by one's Parents', i.e., One's Biological, Physiological, what's more, Inherent psychological Makeup. The Heredity approach feels that the personality of an individual is the Molecular Structure of the qualities, situated in the chromosomes.

Condition

Culture assumes a significant job in the development of personality, i.e., newmolding, the standards among the family, companions, and social gatherings. With the socialization process in the audience, characters are changed after some time.

Circumstance

Although an individual personality is consistent, it changes relying upon the situation. Multiple requests at various times call forward different parts of one's personality.

The relationship between these three components influences the arrangement and improvement of

Personality. Mental legacy is altogether an internal commitment. Gathering andculture are the first ecological elements that structure later behavior.

Family andsocial setting during the beginning times of training are the significant elements which impact the underlying arrangement of personality. Whatever the kid learns here goes on for a lifetime. Sometime down the road, it is the Peer gatherings or Primary affiliations at work, social exercises that shape the Personality.

TYPE AND TRAIT APPROACHES TO PERSONALITY

The conventional saw individuals as Shy, Lazy, Melancholy, Ambitious, Forceful. These were known as Traits. The types of personalities gathered these characteristics.

Trait Approach

Cattel (1973) distinguished 16 source traits/Primary Traits. These characteristics were said to be broadly enduring and consistent sources of conduct. But no logical relevance was seen.

In the approach type, a couple of behaviors are considered high-force men.

Locus of control: People are considered to be of two types: 'Internals' and 'Externals.'

Internals are people who accept that their destiny restricts something that hits them. External people recognize that many of the events have external forces constrained.

Machiavellianism: High Machs will, in general, take control, particularly in approximately organized circumstances; Low Machs react well to oriented situations.

High Machs will, in general, be increasingly sensible, reasonable, and Pragmatic. They become more and more talented to affect and build alliances.

Type 'An' or Type 'B'

People who drive with hardness, enthusiasm, strength, and aggression are called the Type "A" person. The individuals who are friendly, agreeable, laid-back, and non-aggressive are called Type 'B' Personality. Type A people will, in general, be very beneficial and buckle down. They are obsessive workers. The negative side of them is that they are fretful, not great cooperative individuals, progressively fractious, have misguided thinking.

Type B people improve on complex assignments, including judgment, precision as opposed tospeed and cooperation.

SPECULATIONS OF PERSONALITY

There are three fundamental suspicions in principle.

1) Personalities are formative in that they are impacted by past and seeks after what's to come

2) All people have the potential for development and change

3) Personality is the totality of an individual's cooperating sub-frameworks

Enthusiastic Orientations

Two fundamental Orientations of People are **extroversion and self-preoccupation.**

The emotional world is organized in the main by self-observers.They search internally at themselves, maintain a strategic distance from 'social contacts and starting a collaboration with others, pulled back,

calm, and appreciate isolation.

Social butterflies are amicable, appreciate a connection with people, are by and large forceful, and express their emotions and thoughts transparently.

Directors should increase their comprehension of themselves and figure out how understanding others can improve them, administrators.

Legitimacy results demonstrated that contemplative person/outgoing individual is extremely relevant to just the uncommon limits. Most individuals will, in general, be ambiverts, that is, they are in the middle introspection and extroversion.

CRITICAL THINKING STYLES

Two essential strides in critical thinking: gathering data and settling on a choice.

Gathering information happens in a continuum from detecting to instinct. In terms of basic leadership, it ranges from 'thinking' to **'feeling' types**.

Detecting type: The individual methodologies the issue in a bit by bit composed way. The individual works relentlessly and persistently with subtleties.

Instinctive type: One who doesn't show a ton of feeling, who can place things in a legitimate request and who can be firm and reasonable.

The inclination type is extremely mindful of others, detests telling people disagreeable things, and inclines toward congruity among people. The cooperation between these two parts of critical thinking brings about four problem-solving types.

The detecting feeling individual likes to gather information deliberately and make choices that consider the requirements of people. This individual is very worried about the great choices that people will acknowledge and execute.

The instinctive inclination individual is similarly worried about the people's side of choices; however,the attention is on new thoughts, which are frequently wide in scope and ailing in subtleties.

Detecting masterminds underscore subtleties and nature of choice. They are not as worried about the people part of an association likewise with a stable choice. Natural deduction likes to handle new and inventive issues, yet make choices essentially on specialized terms. They will, in general, be great organizers, however not great at executing.

There is constantly a blend of these types in an individual.

General dispositions: The last personality sub-framework Jung recognized was general disposition work, in particular, judging and insightful. Deciding on types like to pursue an arrangement,

Like to decide and need fundamentals for their work. Then again, insightful types adjust well to change, need to understand a vocation thoroughly, and may get overcommitted.

Advancement of Personality:

Distinguished Eight Phases of life that portray the unending improvement of anindividual. It described a specific clash that should be settledeffectively before an individual can move to the following stage. In any case, These eight phases are not separate, and the emergencies are rarely completely settled. Development between stages is formative. Development can even include relapse to prior stages at the point when awful mishaps happen.

STAGE ONE

Infancy

During the primary year of life, an individual purposes the fundamental emergency of trust versus doubt. A baby who Learns in a cherishing and warm way learns to confide in others. Absence of adoration and friendship brings about a question. This stage makes a genuine effect on a kid that impacts occasions for residual life.

STAGE TWO

Early Childhood

In the second and third long stretches of life, a youngster starts to declare freedom. If it is not possible for the youth to control these life parts that the young person is empowered to control, then it will create a sense of self-government. If the youngster experiences steady dissatisfaction or conflicting standard setting, a feeling of self-question, furthermore, disgrace is probably going to create.

STAGE THREE

Play Age

The four-year-olds try to find out what exactly they can do. If it is not possible to encourage a young person to strive for realistic goals, he will develop a sense of activity. If a kid is also blocked, made to feel unfit, the person in question will build up a feeling of 'blame and absence of self-confidence.'

STAGE FOUR

School Age

A child learns numerous new skills from 6 to 12 years of age and creates social capacity. If a kid encounters genuine advancement at a rate good withhis or her capacities, the kid will build up a feeling of industry. The invert circumstance brings about a feeling of inadequacy.

STAGE FIVE

Puberty

The emergency of the high school years increases a feeling of personality as opposed to getting befuddled about what your identity is. While experiencing quick natural changes, the young person is additionally attempting to build up himself or herself as socially discrete from guardians. The self-sufficiency, activity, and industry created in prior stages are significant in helping the adolescent effectively resolve this emergency and plan for adulthood.

STAGE SIX

Youthful Adulthood

The youthful grown-up (the '20s and '30s) faces the emergency of closeness versus disconnection. The feeling of personality created during high school years enables the youthful grown-up to start growing profound and enduring connections.

STAGE SEVEN

Adulthood

We face the crisis of generativity and self-ingestion during their 40's and 50's grown-ups. Self-ingested people never build up a capacity to look past themselves. They may get consumed in professional successes and support, and they may never figure out how to worry about people in the future, the welfare of associations to which they have a place, or the welfare of society in general.

Generative people consider them to be a lot greater than themselves. Profitability in work or kid raising or cultural progression becomes critical to them. Through development and innovativeness, they start to apply the impact that advantages their association.

STAGE EIGHT

Later Life

The grown-up of trustworthiness has increased a feeling of insight and forthcoming that can genuinely help control people in the future.

SIGNIFICANCE OF PERSONALITY

An understanding of personality is important because it can help with the faculty's choices by identifying what qualities are needed to achieve a powerful profession. By expanding an understanding of how personality and employment qualities work together, it can lead to better contracting, transformation, and promotion options and by giving a body of knowledge to improve the personality.

Certain methods can predict characters

Rating Scales' from companions or companions help in foreseeing the behavior.

'Exploratory techniques which help in the evaluation of certain qualities of the individual.

With the assistance of 'Poll,'one can evaluate the behavior of the other, gave the appropriate responses are certifiable. Projective Tests like Thematic Appreciation Test, Rorschach's Ink-Blot test help in foreseeing the personality of an individual,these measures help in the viability of the association.

Frames of mind

Frames of mind are a method for reacting either well or ominously to objects, people, ideas, and so on. They are evaluative proclamations. They reflect how one feels about something. Mentalities are known by behavior. It is a unidimensional variable, i.e., positive or negative.

They are speculative builds. It is something inside an individual. It might be watched, yet the frame of the mind itself can't.

Mentalities in an individual could be seen in three different ways:

1) Direct involvement in the individual or circumstance.

2) Association with other comparable people or circumstances.

3) Gaining from others their relationship with the individual or circumstance.

Direct experience is a solid experience phase of learning. Affiliation is like dynamic conceptualization and speculation.

Moreover, the gain from others is like reflection. Mind frames progress from recognition and the process of learning. There is no introduction to the world with attitudes, but life meets them. However, some basic confidence or question arises at the earliest stages.

On the off chance that a youngster's essential needs arein a caring way, the youngster will build up a feeling of trust generally a feeling of question creates.

The youngster likewise builds up a feeling of self-governance or disgrace and uncertainty.

Each affects our actions.What's more, this linkage to behavior is the thing that administrators are worried about; and they likewise will, in general, comprehend the manners by which behavior influencesmentalities.

ATTITUDES AND ORGANIZATION

In associations, mentalities are significant because they influence the activity behavior. These work-related dispositions top positive or negative assessments that representatives hold about parts of their workplace. There are three essential mentalities; work fulfillment, work contribution, and authoritative duty.

Occupation fulfillment alludes to an individual's general mentality towards their activity, which is either positive or negative, i.e., fulfilled or disappointed.

Occupation inclusion gauges how much an individual relates to his activity effectively takes an interest in it and considers his exhibition imperative to his self-worth. Authoritative responsibility is a guiding principle in terms of unwavering, personality, and association. These mental frameworks are estimated to anticipate behaviors such as efficiency, failure to appear, and sales.

Administrators need not be intrigued distinctly with regards to understanding the mentalities of the people, yet likewise in evolving them. When regulations are available, this may be changed. For changing provisions, powerful exchanges are needed mental analysis is, however, postponed because the convictions and qualities are deeply situated.

Qualities

Qualities are including ideas. American Management Association demonstrated that qualities are at the center of personality and that they are ground-breaking, however quiet power influencing behavior.

Qualities are introduced to allow for a very strong deduction of people's behavior and their interaction. Yet principles are a strong power in humans. What "seems to be in some way" a worker's odd behavior can be well understood if the managers grasp the essential qualities of this behavior.

Rokeach (1973) "values speak to essential feelings that a particular method of lead or on the other hand, end-reality is actually or socially desirable over an inverse or chat method of lead or end-reality."

Rokeach isolated qualities into two general classifications: 'Terminal qualities" identify with finishes to be accomplished, for example, agreeable life, family security, self-regard, and feeling of achievement. 'Instrumental qualities' identify with implies for accomplishing wanted closures, for example, aspiration, fortitude, trustworthiness, and creative mind. Terminal qualities reflect what an individual is, at last, endeavoring to accomplish, while instrumental qualities reflect how the individual arrives.

Qualities implanted to such an extent that it very well may be surmised from people's behavior and their discernment, personality, and inspiration. They, for the most part, impact behavior.

They are moderately steady and persevering. That's because of the way they were learned initially.

Hypothetical - Places high significance on the disclosure of truth through basic, furthermore, judicious methodology.

Monetary - Emphasizes to be valuable and viable.

Stylish - Places the most noteworthy incentive on structure and concordance.

Social - The most elevated worth is given to the adoration for people.

Political -Emphasis is placed on intensity and impact securing.

Strict -It is all about the unity between world interactions and knowledge.People in various occupations place distinctive significance on the six worth types.

The information that people have various types of qualities has driven a couple of the more dynamically oversaw associations to start endeavors to improve the qualities - work fit to upgrade representative execution and fulfillment.

Texas Instruments for occurrence has built up a program to analyze diverse worth types and to coordinate these types appropriately with suitable workplaces inside their organization.

A few individuals, for instance, are named "tribalistic."

- people who need solid, order authority from their supervisors; some are " egocentric" craving individual duties and needing to function as sweethearts in a pioneering style;

some are "Social-focused " looking for principally the social relationship that activity gives, what's more, some are "existential," looking for full articulation of development and self-satisfaction needs through their work, much as a craftsman does.

Charles Hughes, Chief Workers ' Officer and Association Improvement of Texas Instruments accepts the range of work to be done in his association to make those diverse types of work so that individual and hierarchical goals are interwoven.

SOCIALIZATION'S INFLUENCE ON PERSONALITY VALUES AND ATTITUDES

Associations play a main consideration in people's lives, and it significantly affects people's personality, qualities, and mentalities. Socialization is the procedure by which an individual adjusts to the workplace and increases devotion and pledge to an association. 'Through this procedure, an individual learns the objectives of the association, the way to accomplish those objectives, a representative's obligations, and acknowledged methods for carrying on in the association. Also, the individual learns theassociation's demeanors and qualities. As the individual gets associated with the association, there is additionally a propensity to adjust to the demeanors and estimations of the association. In this manner, the association impacts the personality, qualities, and demeanors of an individual.

Pre-appearance arrangements: Individuals create assumptions about an association dependent on past training, work encounters, and contacts with the association.

Experience with the Organization: An individual's underlying direction, preparing, and encounters with different workers who show the acknowledged frames of mind in the association all impact and change the individual.

Personal change and new structures of thinking and skills acquired:

At the point when an individual work in an organization, the person in question continuously realizes what is normal, furthermore, start to build up another personality that is reliable with the association depending, the individual works for sometime in a similar association.

Qualities are introduced to allow for a very strong deduction of people's behavior and their interaction. Yet principles are a strong power in humans. What "seems to be in some way" a worker's odd behavior can be well understood if the managers grasp the essential qualities of this behavior.Socialization happens each time the worker makes a move in an association. As people move vertically up the association's chain of importance, they experience extraordinary standards, qualities, and dispositions. At the passage organize, representatives must absorb these new factors if they are to be fruitful, and the potential is there for a modification of their personality.

Monetary conditions, rivalries, and innovative advances can cause anassociation to change its fundamental direction: The subsequent adjustment will bring new powers to hold up under on every association part - powers which may adjust characters

Schein Socialization Model

Defiance: The new worker could endeavor to battle the association. The outcome may be rejection, or change in the association, or change in the individual (despite whether the individual successes or misfortunes).

Inventive individuality: Where a worker recognizes and rejects the qualities of the association, mental frameworks are also important. In connection with the association, workers use a mixture of individual and authoritative qualities.

Adjust: An individual could comply with the hierarchical powers and apply almost no impact on the association.

Along these lines, socialization is a procedure that applies an impact toward evolving personality.

Be that as it may, pass socialization, learning, and demeanor arrangement make powers that work to keep up personality as a steady type. Perceptual procedure channels socialization powers trying to keep up consistency between people's environment and their self-idea, and it relies upon quality 'of these powers. Personality, Attitude, and Qualities proceed to create and advance over time. To comprehend the procedure of socialization is fundamental for a chief since it relates straightforwardly to the work association.

Outline

From this Unit, it found out that understanding human behavior is fundamental for a viable chief, as it encourages to accomplish hierarchical objectives better. The reasons for individual contrasts and approaches to understanding human behavior are clarified. It was comprehended from this unit, that frames of mind are suppositions about things. Qualities speak to profound situated models by which people assess their reality. The past plays a significant job in the improvement of frames of mind and qualities. Personality is the outcome of an individual's encounters and hereditary impacts. Approaches, speculations, and determinants of personality were clarified. Finally, the socialization process in an association was discussed, which changes the personality, qualities, and mentalities.

DO START WITH PEOPLES YOU KNOW

It tends to be simpler to begin reading the people you know before proceeding onward to outsiders.

These are people that you know things about, and when you take a gander at them, you can presumably observe things that show those traits.

If your closest companion is overly bubbly and agreeable to everybody, you can most likely take a gander at them and get on that trait. Step up and see them, see what it is about them that shows others they are bubbly and well disposed and afterward search for those traits in others around you.

The equivalent is valid for a wide range of traits. By taking in what to search for from people who you definitely know have those traits, you're setting yourself up shockingly better for progress.

You'll find out about various things that part with something about an individual, and you'll gradually have the option to stir your way up to a portion of the more dark actualities and highlights about people in this strategy.

Furthermore, you will have no issue working with complete outsiders either. Your companions and family members are the simple part. At the point when you can peruse your chief and realize when to request that raise will be the troublesome one.

Getting Help Reading People

Reading people is significant expertise to learn. For the vast majority, you likely take a gander at is an 'accept the only choice available' situation, correct? You figure on the off chance that I can understand people, at that point incredible, however, if I can't well, no mischief made, isn't that so? Reading people causes you to be very much a superior person. It encourages you to be a superior person too, which is why it's important to know whether you have a simple understanding or an increasingly wide understanding.

If you don't see how to understand people, it's an ability that you unquestionably can learn. It's something that you can take a shot at for yourself by just returning to those long childhood periods of making stories for the people strolling by. But on the other hand, it's something that you can expand on much further if you propel yourself. The key is ensuring that you don't stop and don't abandon the advancement you're making. You might be shocked exactly the amount you can learn in a short measure of time if you propel yourself on these aptitudes, in any event, beginning with people you know.

The Most Effective Method To Read A Person

It's conceivable to peruse an individual if you give close consideration to their body language, what they state, how they state it, and your instinct and sentiments.

You can never know an individual's contemplations without a doubt. However, you can pick up pieces of information about their considerations and personality by utilizing a couple of key methodologies.

TECHNIQUE 1: READING BODY LANGUAGE

1. Study act

Stance can give numerous insights about what an individual is truly thinking. How they sit and how they lean recounts to a story.

Somewhere in the range of 70 and 90 percent of correspondence can be non-verbal.

- If an individual inclines from you, they are most likely feeling pressure.

- If they are reclining as though they are loose, it tends to be a marker that they feel amazing and in charge.

- Poor stance can imply that an individual needs self-regard or harbors negative sentiments.

2. Recognize positive body language

Specialists separate body language into positive and negative development classes. You can distinguish whether an individual feels positively toward you by spotting positive body language moves.

- Not crossing arms or legs demonstrates positive sentiments.

- Looking ceaselessly, as though timid, is an indication of positive feeling toward you.

- Leaning toward you is a positive body language development.

3. Distinguish negative body language

Certain signs ought to demonstrate to you that the individual may harbor negative sentiments toward you or themselves

- Crossing arms or legs is a development that shows watchfulness

- Pointing feet away or toward a leave implies an individual may have negative emotions

- Looking sideways or sloping forever is a sign of negative body language

- When an individual contacts their nose, eyes, or back of the neck, it can demonstrate negative sentiments

4. Spot counterfeit smiles

Some signs demonstrate an individual's smile isn't certifiable. In a veritable smile, you will see the wrinkles around an individual's eyes. In a phony smile, you frequently won't.

- Smiling uses facial muscles more and more

- The chuckle lines or wrinkles around the eye are brought about by the orbicularis oculi and are muscles enacted in certifiable smiles

- Fast smiles are less inclined to be real

- Fake smiles are sometimes greater because the individual is attempting to extend their face

5. Peruse an individual's eyes

The eyes are expressive, and it's conceivable to educate a ton regarding an individual on the off chance that you recognize what to search for in them.

- Dilated understudies demonstrate intrigue

- Power looking methods an individual investigates the triangle from your eyes to your brow, which means they are keeping away from closeness. If they look from your eyes to your mouth and down, that demonstrates - a longing for closeness. Looking from the eyes to the mouth just is called social looking and shows solace and companionship.

- Sustained eye to eye connection can show endeavor to command or can part with that an individual is lying

- Before turning away, eye contact for a few seconds indicates certainty. For 1 second or less, the eye-to-eye connection indicates an avoidance of uncertainty

- Fast squinting can be a sign an individual is keen on you.

- Liars will regularly look to one side when thinking. A few specialists accept this is because they are preparing a story.

- Closing the eyes for a continued timeframe implies an individual needs time to think.

6. Peruse an individual's hands

Similarly, as with the eyes, the hands can give you pieces of information about an individual's personality or what they are thinking.

- When an individual holds their palms down, it demonstrates they feel ground-breaking. A descending palm can likewise be an indication that something is being dismissed or halted.

- When an individual keeps their palms up, it can demonstrate accommodation. Upward palms likewise show giving and advertising.

7. Understand motions and contact

What people do with their hands can give you signs about what they are thinking. Movements are defined as physical development that reveals feelings or findings.

- When somebody contacts your hand quickly, it shows they need an association with you.

- When an individual rubs their nose, they may be lying.

• If an individual shrouds their hands, they may be concealing something from you.

• When an individual lays their jawline on their hand, they're settling on a choice.

• Scratching the rear of the neck implies an individual has unanswered inquiries.

• Watch out for reflecting signals. At the point when an individual begins to duplicate your appearances and motions, it typically implies they need to sell you something

• Moving into individual space can be an indication of terrorizing

• Raising the eyebrows implies an individual contemplates you and needs to impart better

8. Understand ears

Numerous people disregard the ears, yet advanced face perusers accept that they can offer intimations to personality.

• Small ears demonstrate meticulousness and assurance

• People with huge ears can be a goal and otherworldly

• People with ears that stick out might be courageous types that are available to attempting new things

• When people have ears that are high on their heads, it can demonstrate they are scholarly and enormous masterminds

STRATEGY 2

1. Study word decision

Words people use can offer pieces of information to their behavior. For instance, if an individual discloses to you, they won "another" grant, this gives some insight that they are uncertain because they needed to guarantee you realized they'd won previously.

•   It reveals to you it is compelling to offer recognition for achievements. It pinpoints a zone of helplessness.

•   Study whether an individual's assertion decision coordinates their body language. Irregularity can be telling.

2 Spot lying.

It's conceivable to spot whether an individual may be lying dependently on what they state. Think about their remarks in setting, however, and consistently know that reading, verbal signs isn't idiot-proof.

- Using an inquiry to address an inquiry gives them more opportunities to make up a story.

- When people include qualifiers like "as far as I could know," they may be lying.

- When people are lying, they will sometimes expel references to themselves, maintaining a strategic distance from the utilization of "I."

- When lying, people sometimes utilize the current state to allude to past occasions.

- Some investigations have discovered that people who utilize increasingly formal discourse may be lying. For instance, they probably won't utilize withdrawals or will utilize titles.

- People who are liable for something will sometimes utilize words that mollify the demonstration. For instance, rather than a word like taking, they may utilize a word like acquire.

3. Focus on the tone and speed of the voice.

The sounds people emit when they talk can be extremely uncovering about their characters.

- People who talk excessively quick and a lot of are generally unreliable or on edge.

- Sighing demonstrates bitterness and disappointment.

- If an individual talk too gradually, they might be discouraged or need suddenness.

- If an individual's voice changes pitch abruptly, they may be lying.

- A redundant manner of speaking shows deception.

- When you pull in a lady, men can change their way of speaking more.

4. Understanding sentence length.

The normal sentence contains between 10 to 15 words. It is known as the "mean length of articulation.

- Longer or shorter sentences than normal means that pressure.

- Some specialists trust you can tell an individual is lying if they stray from the mean length of articulation essentially. They will single out those sentences to examine all the more intently.

Strategy 3:

READING EMOTIONAL ENERGY

1. Shake hands.

When you shake a person's hands, what's your feeling of their energy? Give careful consideration of what you feel. Do you feel warmth or chilliness?

- Chinese drug has a word for the energy a person radiates: Chi.

- Another word for emotional energy is a person's "vibe."

- To evaluate a person's energy, you may need to contact them through an embrace or handshake or just by contacting their hand.

2 Use your instinct

Don't overthink it. Is the person feeling better or not? You sometimes need to focus on a "hunch."

- Goose knocks can be a physical sign the body gives you that discloses to you something isn't right. Or on the other hand, they may very well demonstrate a feeling of history repeating itself.]

- Does a person make you feel depleted or stimulated? This provides information about their emotional atmosphere.

- Pay consideration regarding flashes of understanding that interfere with your reasoning.

- What's your feeling of a person's general energy? Not a signal or tone anywhere, yet the general climate they make and feeling they radiate?

3. Lock your eyes

Emotional energy radiates through in the eyes and look. The adage "the eyes are the spirit window" was deliberately made.

• Are they look hard and furious or delicate and inviting?

• With a simple look, intimacy can be achieved. Take carefully into account the body language around your eyes.

4. Read a person's energy type

Antiquated masterminds created five components to depict a person's general energy. They thought understanding these components could assist you with reading people and even spot sickness.

- People with fire energy are showy, crazy, and energizing

- A person who has wood energy is essential, new, and vivacious

- People with earth energy are down to earth and precise

- People with mental energy are discouraged and pulled back

- Water energy is a pointer of tranquillity and objectivity

THE ART OF EFFECTIVE QUESTIONING

Successful inquiries are questions that are incredible and interesting. Successful inquiries are open-finished and not driving inquiries. They are not "why" questions, yet rather "what" or "how" questions. "Why" questions are useful for requesting data, yet can make people protective, so be astute in your utilization of them. When posing successful inquiries, it is critical to hang tight for the appropriate response and not give the appropriate response.

When working with people to tackle an issue, it isn't sufficient to disclose to them what the issue is. They have to discover or comprehend it for themselves. You assist them with doing this by asking them interesting inquiries. As opposed to making suspicions discover what the person you are talking to thinks about the issue.

For instance: "What do you think the issue is?"

The ability to adjust to the appropriate response and suspend judgment is additionally behind the successful approach.So we are committed to understanding what the speaker says. What're their words behind? Restore your feelings to ensure that more data are not adapted for you. Concentrate on your intestines for more information.

Tuning in as Part of Effective Questioning

The customer comes to you, not just for your capacity to win a claim, to arrange a settlement, or draft a report, yet additionally for your knowledge.

You proof your comprehension or shrewdness by tuning in to your customer, not simply posing inquiries or conveying the administration.

As consumers are familiar with it, they feel respected and trust you all the more.

Viable listening is an aptitude that requires sustaining and needs improvement.

Since legal advisors are savvy, the allurement is to get by with tuning in at a negligible level. To interface with your customers and have them experience you as a compelling legal advisor expects you to keep up predominant listening abilities alongside posing powerful inquiries.

Elements that may neutralize powerful listening include:

A craving to keep control of the conversation.

As exceptionally prepared experts, legal counselors need to show their knowledge and aptitudes, so they regularly need to offer a response before they have completely heard the inquiry.

Hearing can give the customer feelings and feelings to hear, and a handful of legal consultants have trouble communicating their feelings and emotions. They think it isn't inside a legal counselor's job or that it is amateurish to do as such.

At the point when we truly tune in to a customer, we start to hear various degrees of correspondence. Getting to a more profound degree of seeing, as opposed to concocting a quick answer, is critical to progressively powerful critical thinking. Tuning, as such, enables the customer to concoct their answer or strategy.

Think about the various accompanying degrees of tuning in:

Level 1 Listening:

At the point when we are tuning in at level 1, our spotlight or consideration is on how the words the other person is stating influence ourselves with insignificant worry for the person talking. We opt for the other person's gestures to see how they affect us. It's about me-what are my feelings, choices, problems, ends, and emotions.There is no room to "connect" the feelings of the person.

Level 2 Listening:

At the point when we tune in at level 2, there is a more profound spotlight on the person being tuned in to. The hearing may make the customers hear their emotions and feelings, and a few lawyers have difficulty communicating their emotions and feelings. Our mindfulness is absolutely on the other person. We notice what they state like how they state it and what they don't state. We tune in for what they esteem and what is essential to them. We tune in for what gives them energy or trouble or abdication. We let go of judgment. We are never again arranging what we are going to state straightaway. We react to what we hear.

Level 3 Listening:

At the point when we listen more profoundly than the two levels depicted above, notwithstanding the conversation, we take in all data that encompasses the conversation. We know about the unique situation and the effect of the setting on all gatherings. We incorporate every one of our faculties, specifically our instinct. What is not said is something we think about, and we notice the energy in the room and in the person we listen to. We utilize that data to pose progressively powerful inquiries.

Listening Skills as a major aspect of Effective Questioning include:

ARTICULATING

Consideration and mindfulness bring about explanation and briefly depicting what we have gained from our customers. Sharing our perception, obviously yet without judgment, does this. We will rehash just what they said to our clients. By articulating to them what we accept they mean, we can develop this.It enables a person to feel heard. "For example, I hear you say."

EXPLAINING

Explaining is a blend of asking and articulating what we have heard. By posing inquiries, our customer realizes we are listening and filling in the holes. At the point when our customer is obscure, it is significant for us to explain the conditions. We can help them to perceive what they can't see themselves by making a recommendation. For instance: "This is what I hear you saying. Is that right?

BEING CURIOUS

Try not to accept you know the appropriate response or what your customer is going to let you know. Pause and be interested in what carries them to see you. What spurs them? What is extremely behind the gathering? Utilize your interest with the goal that your next question can go further.

Quiet Giving the person we are listening to time to respond to questions is a significant part of listening. Trusting that the customer will talk as opposed to talking for them is basic for a compelling audience.

Addressing Techniques

Trash in, trash out," is a prevalent truth, regularly said in connection to PC frameworks: if you put an inappropriate data in, you'll misunderstand the data out.

A similar rule applies to correspondences all in all: on the off chance that you pose an inappropriate inquiry, you'll presumably misunderstand the appropriate response, or if nothing else, not exactly what you're seeking after.

Posing the correct inquiry is at the core of compelling interchanges and data trade. By utilizing the correct inquiries in a specific circumstance, you can improve an entire scope of correspondences' abilities. For instance, you can assemble better data and find out additional; you can manufacture more grounded connections, oversee people all the more viably, and help other people to adopt as well.

Open and Closed Questions

A shut inquiry, as a rule, gets a solitary word or extremely short, truthful answer. For instance, "Are you parched?" The appropriate response is "Yes" or "No"; "Where do you live?" The appropriate response is commonly the name of your town or your location.

Open inquiries evoke longer answers. They normally start with what, why, how. An open inquiry poses to the respondent for their insight, conclusion, or emotions. "Let me know" and "depict" can likewise be utilized similarly as open inquiries. Here are a few models:

- What occurred at the gathering?
- For what reason did he respond that way?
- How was the gathering?

Reveal to me what occurred straightaway. Portray the conditions in more detail.

Open inquiries are useful for:

- Building up an open conversation: "What did you get up to on an excursion?"
- Discovering more detail: "What else do we have to do to make this a triumph?"
- Discovering the other person's assessment or issues: "What's your opinion about those changes?"

Shut inquiries are useful for:

- Testing your comprehension, or the other person's: "All in all, if I get this capability, I will get a raise?"

- Finishing up a dialogue or settling on a choice: "Presently we know the realities, would we say we have altogether concurred this is the correct strategy?"

- Edge setting: "Would you say you are content with the administration from your bank?"

A lost shut inquiry, then again, can execute the conversation and lead to cumbersome quiets, so are best maintained a strategic distance from when a conversation is in full stream.

Driving or 'Stacked' Questions

The main inquiry, typically unobtrusively, focuses the respondent's answer a specific way.

Asking a worker, 'How are you continuing ahead with the new fund framework?' This inquiry prompts the person to address how they are making do with another framework at work. Inconspicuously, it raises the possibility that perhaps they are not finding the new framework so great.

' Tell me how you continue to implement the new account system ' is a less pushing question – no decision required in the inquiry so, therefore, there could be no major challenge with the new account framework.

Youngsters are especially helpless to driving inquiries and are bound to lead the pack for an answer from a grown-up. Something straightforward like, 'Did you have a decent day at school?' focuses the kid towards pondering beneficial things that occurred at school. By asking, 'How was school today?' you are not requesting any judgment about how positive or negative the day has been, and you are bound to get an increasingly adjusted, precise answer. The rest of the conversation can form, and the next question could be, ' What did you do in school? ' The answer to this may vary depending on the basic question you posed – beneficial things or just things.

Review and Process Questions

Questions can likewise be ordered by whether they are 'review' – expecting something to be recollected or reviewed, or 'process' – requiring some more profound idea and additionally investigation.

A basic review question could be, 'What is your mom's original last name?'. That means the respondent must examine some memory data, a reality. A teacher may ask review inquiries of their students, 'What is the most noteworthy mountain?' Process questions require more idea and examination or potentially an imparting of insight. Models incorporate, What aptitudes would you be able to bring to this association that different candidates can't?' or 'What are the points of interest and disservices of posing driving inquiries to youngsters?

Non-serious Questions

Non-serious inquiries are regularly clever and don't require an answer.

'If you set out to flop and, at that point, succeed, have you fizzled or succeeded?' Rhetorical inquiries are regularly utilized by speakers in introductions to get the group of spectators to think — non-serious inquiries are, by configuration, used to advance the idea.

Government officials, teachers, ministers, and others may utilize facetious inquiries while tending to huge spectators to help keep consideration. Who could not remain ata mature age with sound?

' It's not a question that needs an answer, but our minds are changed to see how we are more and more connected to the speaker.

Channeling

We can utilize astute addressing to pipe the respondent's answers – that poses a progression of inquiries that become more (or less) prohibitive at each progression, beginning with open inquiries and consummation with shut inquiries or the other way around.

For instance:

"Educate me regarding your latest occasion.

- "What did you see while you were there?
- "Were there any great cafés?
- "Did you attempt some nearby indulgences?
- "Did you attempt the Clam Chowder?

The inquiries in this model become progressively prohibitive, beginning with open inquiries which take into account wide answers, at each progression, the inquiries become increasingly engaged, and the appropriate responses become progressively prohibitive.

Channeling can work differently, shut inquiries, and working down to progressively open inquiries. For an advisor or examiner, these piping procedures can be a helpful strategy to discover the most extreme measure of data, by starting with open inquiries and afterward progressing in the direction of progressively shut inquiries. Interestingly, when meeting somebody new, it isn't unexpected to begin by posing progressively shut inquiries and advancing to open inquiries as the two gatherings unwind.

Standards for successful addressing

1. Plan to utilize addresses that energize thinking and thinking.

Extremely viable applications scheduled beforehand. It is beneficial to model a series of inquiries that expand the thinking of undergraduates and widen them. Astrong examiner is adaptable and gives time to catch up.

Imparting ends and reflecting

*   What strategy did you use?

*   What different strategies have you considered?

2. Pose inquiries in manners that incorporate everybody

It is important to remember that everyone acknowledges the investigations that have taken place.

Here are three different ways that educators have attempted to accomplish this:

• Use a 'no hands up' rule. After a couple of hands have gone up, certain understudies quit thinking since they realize that the educator won't ask them. At the point when understudies have their hands up, they also quit intuition as they as of now have the appropriate response they need. 'No hands up' urges everybody to continue thinking as anybody might be called upon to react.

• Ask questions that empower a scope of reactions. As opposed to requesting explicit right answers, request thoughts and recommendations: "How might we begin on this?", "What do you notice about this?" Everyone will, at that point, have the option to offer a reaction.

• Avoid educator - understudy - instructor - understudy 'ping pong.' Urge understudies to tune in to and to answer to one another's reactions. Go for an example progressively like: educator - understudy A - understudy B - understudy C - instructor.

•	Arrange the space to energize support. Consider where understudies are sitting – are there some who can't hear? Would students be able to see and hear each other with the goal that they can react to the focuses another understudy makes? It is regularly better to sit understudies in a U-shape, if conceivable.

3. Give understudies time to think

The time interim between an instructor posing an inquiry and providing the appropriate response herself, or catching up with an extra question or remark, is regularly called 'hold up time.' For some instructors, the mean hold up time is short of what one second (Rowe (1974)1). At the point when instructors increment this hold-up time to somewhere in the range of three and five seconds.

The exploration shows that understudies start to:

•	Respond at more prominent length and with more noteworthy certainty;

•	Offer progressively spontaneous, however fitting, reactions;

- Offer progressively different, elective clarifications;

- Relate reactions to those from different understudies. Expanding hold up time is troublesome. Quiet in a homeroom can be difficult to tolerate!

- Talk to understudies about 'hold up time.' Ensure that understudies realize that they should set aside some effort to think before reacting. (A few educators even make themselves hold up by tallying gradually to themselves: "One, two, three, four, got the opportunity to hold up somewhat more"!)

- Use "Think - Pair – Share."Put your investigation, give 10 seconds of thought and then allow 30 seconds to talk to an accomplice. Everyone should then be prepared and know that everyone can be told what they think.

- Use smaller than normal whiteboards. Request that the understudies go through 30 seconds pondering the issue and writing thoughts for the arrangement onto their scaled-down whiteboards. At that point, request that the understudies share the thoughts they had for beginning the issue.

4. Abstain from deciding understudies' reactions

Curiously, Rowe (1974) found that if an educator made judgmental remarks, even positive ones, for example, "Very much done!", at that point, this contrarily influenced understudies' verbal exhibition even with the stretched hold up times.

Errand's determination was most noteworthy, where verbal prizes were less. At the point when an educator makes a decision about each reaction with 'yes,' 'great,' 'almost, etc., understudies are probably going to motivation to themselves:

"The instructor said that was great. That isn't what I was going to state. So what I was going to state can't be great. So I won't utter a word."

Pose open inquiries that license a more noteworthy assortment of reactions and answer to understudies with remarks that don't shut off elective thoughts.

"Much obliged to you for that, that is truly fascinating. What different thoughts do people have?"

5. Follow up understudies' reactions in manners that empower further reasoning

The accompanying methodologies energize further reasoning and exchange:

Request that understudies rehash their clarification

•	Can you state that once more? Welcome understudies to expand

•	Can you say somewhat more regarding that Challenge understudies to offer an explanation

•	Can you clarify why that works? Prompt elective reactions

•	Can you recommend another method for doing this? Backing with non-verbal intrigue

•	Nod head, pivot hand to demonstrate that you need more Urge understudies to theorize.

•	What if? What if? And harsh gestures.

•	Someone in this gathering said, would they say they were correct? Permit practice of reactions

•	Try out the appropriate response on your accomplice first. Urge understudies to pose inquiries

•	Would anybody like to pose Pat an inquiry about that? Request that understudies verbally process

- Can you experience that bit by bit? Urge understudies to make associations

- Can you remember something different we liked this? Verbally processing with understudies

- Let's thoroughly consider this together.

Anticipating compelling addressing

Plan how you will orchestrate the room and the assets required.

Orchestrate understudies with the goal that they can see and hear each other just as the instructor. You may need to adjust seats in a U shape, or the understudies could move and 'roost' closer together. Or on the other hand, possibly, you will move to the rear of the room with the goal that the inquiry is the focal point of consideration and not the educator.

Plan how you will present the scrutinizing session

Quiet will be difficult for you to tolerate in the study hall, yet the understudies may discover it confusing or in any event, compromising. Clarify why there will be times of calm.

Plan how you will set up the standard procedures

On the off chance that you are utilizing 'No hands up' at that point, you should disclose this to the understudies. A few educators have needed to request that their understudies neglect to move, so they recollect not to put their hands up.

The understudies will be permitted to put their hands up to pose an inquiry, so if a hand shoots up,to make sure to pose them what inquiry they might want to inquire. The understudies may likewise be accustomed to offering short responses so you could present a base length rule, for example, 'your answer must be five words long as a base.'

Plan the principal question that you will utilize

Plan the principal question and consider how you will proceed.It is unable to be anticipated because, for instance, it relies on the right answers that you will receive one response and then receive information about your thought. Without a comment, you'll answer a few questions that ask the next person to provide equivalent or specific information about those answers.

Plan how you will give thinking time

• Will you permit 3-5 seconds between posing an inquiry and anticipating an answer?

• Will you request that the understudies think – pair – share, giving 30 seconds for talking to an accomplice before offering a thought in entire class discourse?

• Will you utilize another methodology that permits the understudies time to think?

Plan how and when you will intercede

Will you have to intercede sooner or later to pull together understudies' consideration or examine various techniques they are utilizing? Have a couple of inquiries prepared to pose to a part path through the exercise to mind their advancement and their learning.

STEP BY STEP INSTRUCTIONS TO READ PEOPLE LIKE A PRO: 16 TRICKS FROM PSYCHOLOGY

The capacity to read people appropriately will fundamentally influence your social, personal, and work life.

You can then change the communication and type of communications to ensure that you can get them in a perfect way when you see how someone else thinks.

It isn't so difficult. It might sound trivial. But you don't have to bother to learn how to read people with any exceptional forces.

Along these lines, here are 17 hints for reading people like an expert:

1. Be goal and receptive

Before you endeavor to read people, you should initially work on having a receptive outlook. Try not to let your feelings and past encounters impact your impressions and suppositions.

On the off chance that you judge people effectively, it will make you misread people. Be objective in moving toward each communication and circumstance.

Rationale alone won't disclose to you the entire anecdote about anybody. You should give up on other essential types of data so you can figure out how to read the significant non-verbal, intuitive prompts that people radiate."

To see somebody unmistakably, you should "stay objective and get data impartially without twisting it."

2. Focus on appearance

Judith Orloff M.D says that when reading others, attempt to see people's appearance. What are they wearing?

They are safe for progress, which shows they are target-oriented? Or, on the other hand, are they wear pants and a shirt, that means comfort?

Do they have a pendant, for example, across or Buddha, which shows their otherworldly qualities? Whatever they wear, you can detect something from it.

Sam Gosling, a personality therapist at the University of Texas and writer of the book Snoop, says that you should focus on "character claims."

These are things people decide to appear with their appearances, for example, a shirt with mottos, tattoos, or rings.

"Personality claims are conscious proclamations we make about our frames of mind, objectives, values, and so on… One of the things that are extremely imperative to remember about character explanations is because these are intentional, numerous people accept we are manipulative with them. We're deceitful, yet I believe there's little proof to propose that that goes on. I think, by and large, people truly would like to be known. They'll even do that to the detriment of looking great. They'd preferably be seen genuinely over positively on the off chance that it came down to that decision."

Likewise, a few discoveries recommend that maybe mental traits can – somewhat – be read on a person's face.

The more projective nose and lips and a latent jaw and masseter muscles (the mandible used to bit) were identified in higher levels of extraversion. However, the essence of people with low extraversion levels revealed the inverted design in which the territory surrounding the nose seemed to push against the face.

3. Focus on people's stance

A person's stance says a great deal regarding their mentality. If they hold their head high, it implies they are confident.

On the off chance that they walk falteringly or fall, it might be an indication of low self-regard.

Judith Orloff M.D says that with regards to pose, search for on the off chance that they confidently hold their high, or on the off chance that they walk ambivalently or fall, which shows low self-regard.

4. Check your physical development

More than words, people express their emotions through developments.

For instance, we lean toward those we like and away from those we don't.

"If they're inclining in if their hands are out and open, palms looking up, that is a decent sign that they are interfacing with you," says EvyPoumpouras, a previous Secret Service specialist.

If you have seen that the person is inclining endlessly, it implies the person is setting up a divider.

Another development to see is the intersection of arms or legs. On the off chance that you see a person doing this, it recommends preventiveness, outrage, or self-insurance.

EvyPoumpouras says that "on the off chance that somebody is inclining in and out of the blue you state something and their arms crossed, presently I realize I said something that this person didn't care for."

Then again, concealing one's hands implies that they are concealing something.

In any case, on the off chance of seeing them picking lip gnawing or fingernail hair, it means they're trying to alleviate themselves under pressure or in a sloppy situation.

5. Attempt to translate outward appearances

Unless you are an as of the poker face, you're going to be cut in.

As indicated by Judith Orloff M.D, there are a few different ways to translate outward appearances. They are:

At the point when you see profound glare lines shaping, it might propose the person is stressed or overthinking.

A person who is genuinely snickering will show crow's feet – the smile lines of bliss.

Another thing to look for is tight lips that can flag up first, contempt and sharpness. Besides, the gripped jaw and crushing of the teeth are pressure indications.

They are:

Prize smile: Lips pulled straightforwardly upwards, dimples along the edges of mouth and eyebrows lift. This gives good feedback.

Affiliative smile: Involves squeezing lips together while additionally making little dimples along the edge of the mouth — an indication of companionship and love.

Predominance smile: The upper lip is raised, the cheeks up, the nose is wrinkled, the space between mouth and nose spreads, and the top cover is raised.

6. Try not to flee from small talk.

Possibly you feel unease with small talk. Be that as it may, it can offer you the chance to acclimate yourself with the other person.

Small talk causes you to see how a person carries on in ordinary circumstances. You would then be able to utilize it as a benchmark to precisely detect any strange behavior.

In The Silent Language of Leaders: How Body Language Can Help–or Hurt–How You Lead, the writer calls attention to various mistakes that people make when attempting to read people, and one of them was that they don't get a pattern of how they ordinarily act.

7. Output the person's general behavior.

Often we expect a person to be apprehensive or anxious if a certain activity takes place, such as looking down at a discussion.

In any case, on the off chance you're already familiar with a person, you'll know if the person is keeping away from eye-to-eye connection or just loosening up when the person in question looks down the floor.

According to LaRaeQuy, an FBI counter-internship operator, "people have different characteristics and behaviors, which can essentially be part of."

That is the reason for making a standard of others' typical behavior will support you.

Figure out how to recognise any deviation from a person's typical behavior. You will realize something isn't right when you notice an adjustment in their tone, pace, or body language.

7. Output the person's general behavior

Occasionally, we agree that if there is a certain event, such as a conversation with the floor, it means that the individual is concerned or on his edge.

Be that as it may, on the off chance that you are already acquainted with a person, you will know whether the person maintains a strategic distance from eye to eye connection or is simply loosening up when the person in question looks down the floor.

According to the LaRaeQuy, the retired counterintelligence expert for the FBI, "people have different traits, indicators of behavior."

That is the reason for making a benchmark of others' ordinary behavior will support you.

Figure out how to distinguish any deviation from a person's typical behavior. You will realize something isn't right when you notice an adjustment in their tone, pace, or body language.

"For instance, if your supervisor says she's "chose to go with brand X," the activity word is chosen. This single word demonstrates that in all likelihood, your manager 1) isn't imprudent, 2) gauged a few choices, and 3) thoroughly considers things. Action words offer bits of knowledge into how a person thinks."

9. Notice the words and tone utilized

At the point when you talk to somebody, attempt to see the words they use. At the point when they state, "This is my subsequent advancement," they need you to realize that they likewise earned an advancement beforehand.

Learn to expect the unexpected. These types of people depend on others to support their self-picture. They need you to adulate them so they will like themselves. You ought to likewise post for the tone utilized: "The tone and volume of our voice can educate much concerning our feelings. Sound frequencies make vibrations. When reading people, notice how their manner of speaking influences you. Ask yourself: Does their tone feel relieving? Or, on the other hand, is it grating, short, or whiny?"

11. Tune in to what your gut says

Tune in to your gut, particularly when you initially meet a person. It will give you an instinctive response before you get an opportunity to think.

Your gut will hand-off whether you're calm or not with the person.

As per Judith Orloff M.D, "Hunches happen rapidly, a base reaction. They're your internal truth meter, transferring on the off chance that you can confide in people."

12. Feel the goosebumps, assuming any

Goosebumps happen when we reverberate with people who move or rouse us. It can likewise happen when a person is stating something that inspires an emotional response inside us.

"At the point when we take a gander at inquiring about [on the chills], outside of the transformative reaction to warm ourselves, it's music that appears to trigger it, just as moving encounters and even motion pictures," said Kevin Gilliland, a Dallas-based clinical analyst.

Furthermore, we feel it when we experience this feels familiar, an acknowledgment that you've known somebody previously. However, you've ever met.

13. Focus on flashes of knowledge

Sometimes, you may get an "ah-ha" minute about people. However, they remain alert because these bits of knowledge arrive instantly.

We will, in general, miss it since we go onto the following idea so quickly that these basic bits of knowledge get lost. Hunches are your internal truth meter:

"Hunches happen rapidly, a basic reaction. They're your internal truth meter, transferring on the off chance that you can confide in people."

14. Since the person's quality

It ensures that we have to sense the total social environment.

At the point when you read people, attempt to see if the person has a benevolent nearness that draws in you or you face a divider, making you back off.

As indicated by Judith Orloff M.D, nearness is:

"This is the general energy we produce, not harmonious with words or behavior."

15. Watch people's eyes

They state our eyes are the entryway to our spirits – they transmit incredible energies. So set aside the effort to watch people's eyes.

When you look, would you be able to see a minding soul? Is it accurate to say that they are mean, furious, or monitored?

As indicated by Scientific American, eyes can "pass on whether we are lying or coming clean."

They can likewise "fill in as a decent finder for what people like" by seeing understudy size.

16. Try not to make suppositions.

This almost leaves saying, but remember that assumptions are mistaken. It is a matter of more concern when you effectively suspect without knowing the person.

In The Silent Language of Leaders: How Body Language Can Help–or Hurt–How You Lead, the writer pointed a few blunders people make when reading others, and one of them was not being aware of predispositions.

For instance, if you expect that your companion is irate, at that point, whatever they state or do will appear covered outrage to you.

Try not to bounce into end when your significant other hit the hay early as opposed to watching your preferred TV appear with you. Possibly she's worn out – don't think she isn't keen on investing energy with you.

The way to reading people like a star is to unwind and keep your mind open and positive.

17. Work on watching people.

Careful learning creates promising results so that the more people you learn, the more effectively you can understand them.

As an activity, an attempt to work on watching talk appears on the quiet. Looking at their physical actions and behaviors can cause you to understand, without having heard phrases, what people feel when they speak.

At that point, watch again with the volume on and check whether you are direct with your perception.

One of the most significant things you can know is the way to read people.

It makes you touchy to the battles and needs of the people around you. It is an aptitude that you can figure out how to additionally help your EQ.

DISCOVERING PATTERNS

The perception of an example is just like a telescope looking. As if you see things you've never seen with new eyes. This equivalent experience could occur just because you see an example.

At the point when you see an example, it can completely change you. Seeing an example can even make you more astute. Examples are amazing. They set up desires, make associations, and move consuming inquiries. They can be occasions that normally rehash themselves, inclines in which occasions rise or fall over a delayed period, connections that make new associations, or they can rise out of observing the bigger picture.

Everybody can be designed shrewd, be that as it may, in various ways. People who are numbers shrewd, for instance, can foresee from a progression of numbers what the following number will be. The individuals who can perceive a type of flying creature from its flight design are nature savvy. Do you see what clever jokes share for all intents and purposes, and would you be able to make one? If you can, you are word keen. People who can picture an item in three measurements are outwardly brilliant. The survey that pursues tests on the off chance that you are people savvy. What number of these would you be able to check, yes?

Can You/Do You

- Distinguish a phony smile from a certifiable smile?

- Identify somebody just by their stride and body pose?

- Predict precisely from reading one's face whether somebody is coming clean?

- Predict somebody's activity execution from their Facebook profile?

- Predict from reading body language and outward appearance what somebody is thinking?

- Identify from watching a kid's social connection that a youngster has uncommon needs?

- Notice that in specific callings, the recurrence of left-gave people is higher than righties?

- Do you know how and why they are sorted out in drug stores and grocery stores?

- Perceive how are peer-pressure impacts purchasing propensities?

- Recognize that grinning for no obvious explanation can make you feel upbeat?

People who exceed expectations at unraveling the significance of human behavior designs are people shrewd. That would incorporate you if you checked yes to the vast majority of the inquiries above. People-keen people frequently share certain attributes. They are touchy to the sentiments of others, great at getting others, and exhibit compassion to other people.

There are hypotheses of example acknowledgment: layout coordinating, prototype-coordinating, include investigation, acknowledgment by-parts hypothesis, base up and top-down handling, and Fourier examination. The use of these speculations in regular daily existence isn't unrelated. Example acknowledgment enables us to read words, get language, perceive companions, and even acknowledge music. The different exercises and rooms where design recognition is monitored apply to all of the speculations. A few areas of this kind are facial, music and language recognition and seriation. Facial recognition and serialization occur through the coding of visual examples, while sound-related examples are coded by music and language recognition.

1. Speculations

- Template matching

The layout coordinating hypothesis depicts the essential way to deal with human example acknowledgment. It is a hypothesis that accepts each apparent item is put away as a "layout" into long haul memory. Approaching data is contrasted with these formats to locate a careful match. All tactile information is contrasted with various portrayals of an article to shape one single reasonable comprehension. The hypothesis characterizes discernment as a fundamentally acknowledgment based procedure. It expects that all that we see, we see just through the past presentation, which at that point illuminates our future observation regarding the external world.

- **Prototype matching**

Dissimilar to the definite, balanced layout coordinating hypothesis, prototype coordinating rather look at approaching tangible contribution to one normal prototype. This hypothesis suggests that presentation to a progression of related boosts prompts the formation of a "run of the mill" prototype dependent on their mutual highlights. It diminishes the quantity of put away layouts by institutionalizing them into a solitary portrayal. The model confirms perceptive adaptability because it is sporadic in identifying new benefits, unlike in design teamwork. For example, if a kid had never observed a folding chair, they would at present have the option to remember it as a seat on account of their comprehension of its fundamental qualities as having four legs and a seat. This thought, be that as it may, limits the conceptualization of items that can't be "found the middle value of" into one, similar to types of canines, for example. Even though pooches, wolves, and foxes are, for the most part, ordinarily hairy, four-legged, modestly estimated creatures with ears and a tail, they are not any different, and in this way can't be carefully seen regarding the prototype coordinating hypothesis.

- **Feature examination**

Numerous speculations attempt to clarify how humans can perceive designs in their condition. Highlight discovery hypothesis suggests that the sensory system sorts and channels approaching improvements to permit the human (or creature) to understand the data. The model confirms perceptive adaptability because it is sporadic in identifying new benefits, unlike in design teamwork. The hypothesis proposes an expanding unpredictability in the connection among indicators and the perceptual element. The essential component indicators react to the basic properties of the upgrades. Further along the perceptual pathway, higher composed element indicators can react to increasingly unpredictable and explicit improvement properties. At the point when highlights rehash or happen in a significant succession, we can recognize these examples in light of our element identification framework.

- **Recognition by segments hypothesis**

As an aspect of the theory of exploration, identification by segments (RBC) revolves around the basis of the developments under supervision. First proposed by Irving Biederman (1987), this hypothesis expresses that humans perceive protests by separating them into their essential 3D geometric shapes called geons (for example, chambers, solid shapes, cones, and so on.). A model is a manner by which we separate a typical thing like an espresso mug: we perceive the empty chamber that holds the fluid and a bent handle off the side that enables us to hold it. Although few out of every odd espresso mug is the equivalent, these fundamental segments encourage us to perceive the consistency crosswise over models (or example).

RBC proposes that there are less than 36 novel geons that, when joined, can shape a boundless number of items.

To parse and dismember an article, RBC proposes we take care of two explicit highlights:

EDGES AND CONCAVITIES.

Edges: empower the onlooker to keep up a predictable portrayal of the item paying little respect to the review edge and lighting conditions.

Concavities: are the place two edges meet and empower the spectator to see where one geon closes and another start.

The RBC standards of visual item acknowledgment can be applied to sound-related language acknowledgment too. Instead of geons, language analysts recommend that communicated in language can be separated into fundamental parts called phonemes, Top-down and base up handling

- **Top-down processing**

Top-down handling alludes to the utilization of foundation data in design acknowledgment. It generally starts with a person's past information and makes expectations because of this already gained information. Analyst Richard Gregory measured that 90% of the numbers were lost in time to go from the brain to the head, which is why the cerebrum has to wonder about what it does in the past.We build our impression of the real world, and these observations are speculations or suggestions dependent on past encounters and put away data. The development of wrong suggestions will prompt blunders of discernment, for example, visual hallucinations. In a passage composed of troubled penetration, it is clearer what the author should allow you to read the whole section rather than to read it alone. The cerebrum might have the option to see and comprehend the essence of the section because of the setting provided by the encompassing words.

- **Bottom-up processing**

Base up preparing is otherwise called information-driven handling, since it begins with the incitement of the tangible receptors. Analyst James Gibson contradicted the top-down model and contended that recognition is immediate and not expose to speculation testing, as Gregory proposed. He expressed that sensation is recognition, and there is no requirement for additional understanding, as there is sufficient data in our condition to comprehend the world immediately.

His hypothesis is sometimes known as the "natural hypothesis" in light of the case that observation can be clarified exclusively as far as the earth. A case of base up-handling includes showing a blossom at the focal point of a person's field. The flower and all upgrade data from the retina to the visual cortex are taken into account. One way is the sign.

2. Seriation

Seriation is the capacity to mastermind things in a coherent request along with a quantitative measurement, for example, length, weight, age, and so forth. It is an intellectual ability that only after the nursery years is fully active. The young man should have the option of addressing the inquiry, "What is right? " to understand that articles can be requested in conjunction with measurement and successfully performed as such, seriating skills also help create critical thinking skills, valuable in the perception and completion.

- **Application of seriation in schools**

To assist work with increasing math aptitudes in youngsters, instructors and guardians can assist them with learning seriation and designing. Small kids who comprehend seriation can take care of numbers from most reduced to most elevated. In the long run, they will come to comprehend that six is higher than 5, and 20 is higher than 10. Essentially, having kids duplicate examples or make examples of their own, as ABAB designs, is an extraordinary method to assist them with perceiving arrange and plan for later math aptitudes, for example, augmentation. Kid care suppliers can start presenting youngsters to designs at a young age by having them make the most of gatherings and the complete number of items

- **Development of critical thinking abilities**

For the development of serial skills, which help to advance critical thinking at this stage, young people should be given the possibility to work together, for example, in the form of "enormously" and "greater" links. They ought to likewise be allowed to orchestrate questions all together dependent on the surface, sound, flavor, and shading. Alongside explicit undertakings of seriation, youngsters ought to be allowed to think about the various materials and toys they use during play. Through exercises like these, the genuine comprehension of attributes of articles will create. To help them at a young age, the contrasts between the items ought to be self-evident. In summary, a gradually intertwined task is also to organize two distinct articles and to see how the two singular sets relate.

3. Facial example acknowledgment

Perceiving faces is one of the most widely recognized types of example, acknowledgment. People have an unimaginable power to find faces, but this simplicity and automaticity give a false representation of an extraordinary problem.All faces are physically comparable. Appearances have two eyes, one mouth, and one nose all in unsurprising areas, yet humans can perceive a face from a few distinct edges and in different lighting conditions.

Neuroscientists set that perceiving faces happens in three stages. The principal stage begins with outwardly concentrating on the physical highlights. The facial acknowledgment framework then needs to recreate the character of the person from past encounters. These give the sign to us; it can be an individual we know. When the face evokes the person's name, the final period of recognition ends.

Even though humans are extraordinary at perceiving faces under typical review edges, topsyturvy faces are enormously hard to perceive. It shows how difficult facial recognition is and how humans can perceive faces under standard up to date conditions with specific systems and capacity. It is true.

- **Neural instruments**

Mind liveliness featuring the fusiform face territory thought to be the place facial handling and acknowledgment happens

Researchers concur that there is a sure region in mind explicitly dedicated to handling faces. This structure is known as the fusiform gyrus, and mind imaging thinks about have indicated that it turns out to be profoundly dynamic when a subject is seeing a face.

A few contextual investigations have revealed that patients with sores or tissue harm confined to this zone have huge trouble perceiving faces, even their own. Albeit a large portion of this exploration is conditional, an examination at Stanford University gave definitive proof to the fusiform gyrus' job in facial acknowledgment. In a special contextual investigation, analysts had the option to send direct motion toward a patient's fusiform gyrus. The patient detailed that the essences of the specialists and medical attendants changed and transformed before him during this electrical incitement. Analysts concur this exhibits a persuading causal connection between this neural structure and the human capacity to perceive faces.

- **Facial acknowledgment advancement**

Even though in grown-ups, facial acknowledgment is quick and programmed, youngsters don't arrive at grown-up levels of execution (in research center assignments) until youthfulness. To establish regularly how facial recognition creates, two general speculations have been advanced. The primary, general subjective advancement hypothesis, recommends that the perceptual capacity to encode faces is completely grown right off the bat in childhood and that the proceeded with the progress of facial acknowledgment into adulthood credited to other general components. These general variables incorporate improved attentional center, intentional errand methodologies, and metacognition. Research underpins the contention that these other general components improve drastically into adulthood. The face-explicit perceptual advancement hypothesis contends that the improved facial acknowledgment among kids and grown-ups is because of an exact improvement of facial recognition. The explanation for this change is a radical engagement in the eyes.

- **Developmental issues**

A few developmental issues show a diminished limit concerning facial acknowledgment. Using what we think of the job of the fusiform gyrus, inquiries indicated that social progress, along with a chemical imbalance, is impaired by the addition of a behavioral marker, in which these persons are generally turning away from the faces. Those who struggle with developmental prosopagnosia (DP) in such a way that they are often unable even to recognize their faces.Numerous examinations report that around 2% of the total populace have developmental prosopagnosia and that individuals with DP have a family ancestry of the trait. Individuals with DP are behaviorally vague from those with physical harm or injuries on the fusiform gyrus, again involving its significance to facial acknowledgment. In spite of those with DP or neurological harm, there stays an enormous fluctuation in facial acknowledgment capacity in the all-out populace. It is obscure what represents the distinctions in facial acknowledgment capacity, regardless of whether it is an organic or environmental air. Late research dissecting indistinguishable and brotherly twins indicated that facial acknowledgment was fundamentally higher corresponded in indistinguishable twins, proposing a solid hereditary segment to individual contrasts in facial acknowledgment capacity.

4. Language advancement

- **Pattern acknowledgment in language procurement**

Recent research has revealed the connection between baby language security and psychological example recognition. In contrast, researchers accept that language has a trained ability to learn and comply with ancient nativist hypotheses of language promotion. Concentrates at the Hebrew University and the University of Sydney both show a solid connection between's capacity to distinguish visual examples and to become familiar with another language. Kids with high shape acknowledgment demonstrated better syntax information, in any event, while controlling for the impacts of insight and memory limit. The theory that language acquisition relies on observable training supports this idea, which implies that newborn children often see mixtures and use them for the development of future discourses.

- **Phonological advancement**

The initial phase in newborn child language obtaining is to decode between the most fundamental sound units of their local language; this includes every consonant, every short vowel sound, and any additional letter mixes in English such as ' th ' and ' ph. ' The introduction and the example acknowledgment recognize the units called phonemes. Newborn children utilize their "inborn element indicator" abilities to recognize the hints of words. They split them into phonemes through a component of straight out recognition. They distinguish factual data by perceiving which sound mixtures are to take place together as "qu" or "h.". Along these lines, their capacity to learn words depends legitimately on the exactness of their prior phonetic designing.

- **Grammar advancement**

The change from phonemic separation into higher-request word creation is just the initial phase in the progressive procurement of language. Example acknowledgment is besides used in the discovery of prosody signs, the pressure, and sound examples among words. The word definition and interpretation of average provisional limits are used at this stage.This whole procedure is reflected in reading also. Initial, a kid, perceives examples of individual letters, at that point words, at that point gatherings of words together, at that point sections, lastly whole parts in books. Figuring out how to read and figuring out how to communicate in a language depends on the "stepwise refinement of examples" in perceptual example acknowledgment.

5. Music pattern acknowledgment

Music gives profound and emotional encounters to the audience. Such conferences become a long-term material, and each time we learn the same tales, they are acted upon. Perceiving the substance by the pattern of the music influences our feeling. Different scientists have considered the element that structures the pattern recognition of music and experience.The sensation felt when listening to our preferred music is apparent by the expansion of the understudies, the expansion in heartbeat and pulse, the gushing of blood to the leg muscles, and the enactment of the cerebellum, the mind area related with physical development. When the mind of a track retrieves the melodic sequence, it also occurs when you listen to a song because of the common understanding of the sound. The repetitive idea of the meter enables the audience to pursue a tune, perceive the meter, anticipate it's up and coming event, and figure the musicality. The energy of following a well-known music pattern happens when the pattern breaks and gets eccentric.

This following and breaking of a pattern make a critical thinking open door for the mind that structure the experience.

Therapist Daniel Levitin contends that the redundancies, melodic nature, and association of this music make importance for the cerebrum. The mind stores data in the course of action of neurons which recover similar data when actuated by the earth. By always referencing data and extra incitement from the earth, the cerebrum builds melodic highlights into a perceptual entirety.

- **Cognitive components**

To comprehend music pattern acknowledgment, we have to comprehend the fundamental intellectual frameworks that each handle a piece of this procedure. Different exercises are grinding away in this acknowledgment of a bit of music and its patterns. Scientists have started to disclose the explanations for the invigorated responses to music. Specialists based in Montreal asked ten volunteers who had "chills" to listen to music to adapt to their main stories while watching their mental movements. The outcomes show the huge job of the core cucumbers (NAcc) district – associated with subjective procedures, for example, inspiration, reward, enslavement, and so forth – making the neural game plans that make up the experience. A sense of payment expectation is created by expectation before the height of the tuna that reaches a sense of objectives when the height is reached. As the audience widens, the more prominent the emotional stimulation is the normal pattern. To analyze this idea, musicologist Leonard Meyer used 50 parts of Beethoven's Fifth String Quartet development in C-sharp minor Op. The greater the basis for this experience, the clearer the memory. This quality is influencing the speed and accuracy of the recovery and recognition of the muscle pattern. The brain perceives not only explicit tones but also standard acoustic highlights, speeches, and music.MIT scientists directed an examination to look at this thought. The outcomes indicated six neural bunches in the sound-related cortex, reacting to the sounds. Four were activated when hearing standard acoustic highlights, one explicitly reacted to discourse, and the last only reacted to the music. Analysts who examined the relationship between's transient advancement of timbral, tonal, and cadenced highlights of music arrived at the resolution that music draws in the cerebrum locales associated with engine activities, feelings, and imagination. The examination shows that the entire mind "illuminates" when listening to music. This measure of movement helps memory safeguarding, subsequently pattern acknowledgment.

Perceiving patterns of music is diverse for an artist and an audience. Albeit an artist may play similar notes unfailingly, the subtleties of the recurrence will consistently be extraordinary. The audience will perceive the melodic pattern and their types regardless of the varieties. These melodic types are theoretical and gotten the hang of, which means they may fluctuate socially. Although members of the audience are interested in perceiving (specific) melodic content, the actors investigate it (unambiguous).

An investigation showed that neurons related to the muscles needed to play the fire instrument when watching or hearing music played. When artists and non-artists tun into a piece, mirror neurons light up.

• **Developmental issues**

Pattern acknowledgment of music can fabricate and reinforce different abilities, for example, melodic synchrony and attentional execution and melodic documentation and mind commitment. Indeed, even a couple of long periods of melodic preparing upgrades memory and consideration levels.

Researchers at the University of Newcastle led an examination on patients with extreme gained mind wounds (ABIs) and solid members, utilizing mainstream music to look at music-evoked personal recollections (MEAMs). The members are approached with melodies to record their character, regardless of their preferences and of the collections they recalled.

The outcomes demonstrated that the ABI patients had the most noteworthy MEAMs, and every one of the members had MEAMs of a person, people, or life period that were commonly positive. The members finished the assignment by using pattern acknowledgment aptitudes. Memory inspiration made the melodies sound progressively commonplace and popular.

This examination can be advantageous to restoring patients of self-portraying amnesia who don't have a fundamental lack of self-portraying review memory and flawless pitch discernment.

6. Bogus pattern acknowledgment

The human inclination to see patterns that don't exist is called apophenia. Models remember the Man for the Moon, faces or figures in shadows, in mists, and in patterns with no conscious plan, for example, the twirls on a prepared dessert, and the impression of causal connections between occasions which are random. Apophenia is unequivocally present in paranoid ideas, betting, measuring confusion and logical information, and in various sorts of strict and paranormal meetings. Misperception of patterns is called pareidolia in unregular information.

LEARNING THE ART AND SECRETS OF NONVERBAL COMMUNICATION

As indicated by specialists, a considerable part of our communication is nonverbal. Consistently, we react to thousands of nonverbal signs and behaviors, including stances, outward appearance, eye stare, signals, and manner of speaking. From our handshakes to our haircuts, nonverbal subtleties uncover what our identity is and sway how we identify with others.

Logical research on nonverbal communication and behavior started with the 1872 distribution of Charles Darwin's The Expression of the Emotions in Man and Animals. Since that time, plenteous research on the types, impacts, and articulations of implicit communication and behavior. While these signs are frequently so unobtrusive that we are not deliberately mindful of them, inquire about has recognized a few unique types of nonverbal communication.

As a rule, we impart data in nonverbal ways utilizing gatherings of behaviors. For instance, we may join a grimace with crossed arms and an unblinking eye stare to show objection.

Nonverbal communication alludes to motions, outward appearances, manner of speaking, eye to eye connection (or deficiency in that department), body language, act, and different ways people can convey without utilizing language.

At the point when you're meeting for an occupation or participating in a gathering, your nonverbal communication is nearly as significant as your verbal reactions. Crossed arms can appear to be protective. The poor stance may seem amateurish. A down look or a strategic distance from eye to eye can be considered confidential.

Bosses will assess what you do just as what you state, and you can utilize your nonverbal communication abilities to establish the best connection. If your abilities aren't first class, you can rehearse them, so you establish a positive connection with everybody you meet in the working environment and past.

Types of Nonverbal Communication

- Eye contact

- Facial articulations

- Gestures

- Posture and body direction

- Body Language

- Space and Distance

- Proximity

- Para-semantic

- Humor

- Touch

- Silence

- Personal Appearance

- Symbol

- Visual Communication

Eye to eye connection

The eyes assume a significant job in nonverbal communication, and such things as looking, gazing, and the flickering is significant nonverbal behaviors. At the point when people experience people or things that they like, the pace of squinting increments and understudies enlarges. Taking a gander at someone else can demonstrate a scope of feelings, including antagonistic vibe, intrigue, and fascination.

People likewise use eye stare as a way to decide whether somebody is being honest.6 Normal, watchful gaze contact is frequently taken as a sign that a person is coming clean and is dependable. Tricky eyes and a failure to keep in touch, then again, is habitually observed as a pointer that somebody is lying or being misleading.

Outward appearances

The first and generally self-evident, piece of information to nonverbal communication is a person's outward appearances.

Even though we have one face, it can show an abundance of appearances. From a half-smile to an all-out grin to an easygoing eye move, our outward appearances show a scope of feelings. Rather than diving into every one of the subtleties like a characteristic of the lip or a jerk of the eye, we should investigate the three most unmistakable articulations:

- Smiling - A smile, by and large, shows bliss or satisfaction

- Scowling - A glower or scowl demonstrates dissatisfaction or disappointment

- Lack of Expression - A passive face can demonstrate, at the very least, two things. To begin with, this can be a sign of a lack of engagement or fatigue. Second, and maybe more regrettable, a vacuous face can demonstrate scorn.

A vacuous face is difficult to translate, so on the off chance that you presume you're displaying what's known as a "stone" face, it may be decent to fly in a delicate smile now and again.

Motions and Movement

While the face is obvious for the state of mind, the whole body is an indicator.

Have you, at any point, watched a warmed discussion through a glass gathering room?

Here is a portion of the things you might've seen:

- Frequent and even wild hand motions

- Finger-pointing

- Arms waving noticeable all around

- Raking fingers through their hair

- Invasion of personal space to communicate something specific of threatening vibe

Then again, if everybody's sitting calmly around a gathering table, you can at present note nonverbal communication signs. Imagine a scenario in which somebody has their arms crossed. They could say, "I am cut off from you and your thoughts," but purposely or accidentally.

On the other hand, if somebody's laying their hands on the table with a loose and open stance, they're passing on a message of transparency and eagerness.

Imagine a scenario where somebody is tinkering with their pen or espresso cup and not taking a gander at the speaker. It could be a sign they're exhausted with the subject. Or then again, it may have nothing to do with the speaker by any means. They might be distracted by their personal lives. In any case, it tends to be a sign they're not completely present.

Strikingly, fiddling is likewise an indication of energy if somebody is tinkering with their pen or espresso cup. But it's completely linked to the speaker and can have a significant energy cost.

For this situation, fiddling is their method for giving a portion of that energy a chance to out. It's sort of like somebody whose leg continues skipping. They're either distracted or loaded with energy and ready to shake.

Stance And Body Direction

Stance and development can likewise pass on a lot of information. Research on body language has developed altogether since the 1970's, however prevalent media have concentrated on the over-elucidation of protective stances, arm-intersection, and leg-crossing.

While these nonverbal behaviors can show emotions and dispositions, examine proposes that body language is unquestionably more unobtrusive and less authoritative than recently accepted.

Standing erect, yet not inflexible, and inclining somewhat forward conveys to understudies that you are congenial, open, and benevolent.

Besides, Interpersonal closeness results when you and your understudies face one another. Talking with your back turned or taking a gander at the floor or roof ought to stay away from; it imparts a lack of engagement to your group.

Body Language

Body language is another generally perceived type of non-verbal communication. Body developments can pass on implications and messages. Body language may take two types of oblivious developments and intentionally controlled developments.

For instance;

At the point when a person is exhausted, he may look around the room as opposed take a gander at the speaker, or he may move positions as often as possible.

At the point when a person is apprehensive, he may chomp his nails or pound hair. They are usually done unconsciously. Then again, inclining forward toward the speaker to express intrigue is the situation of cognizant body developments.

Space And Distance

Space and separation are critical non-verbal apparatuses on account of hierarchical communication.

An extensive and well-adorned room shows a person's situation in the association chain of command, and external people get a message about his significance and authority just by visiting his room.

Separation is another communication apparatus, which communicates the level of closeness and individual acknowledgement.

Nearness

Social standards direct an agreeable separation for communication with understudies.

You should search for a sign of inconvenience brought about by attacking understudies' space.

A portion of these are:

- Rocking

- Leg swinging

- Tapping

- Gaze revolution

Regularly, in huge school classes, space attack isn't an issue. There is normally an excess of separation.

To check this, move around the study hall to expand communication with your understudies.

Expanding nearness empowers you to look and builds the open doors for understudies to talk.

Para-semantic

This feature of nonverbal communication incorporates such vocal components as:

- Tone

- Pitch

- Rhythm

- Timbre

- Loudness

- Inflexion

For most extreme showing adequacy, learn to differ these six components of your voice.

One of the significant reactions is of educators who talk in a monotone. Audience members see these teachers as exhausting and dull.

Understudies report that they learn less and lose premium all the more immediately when listening to educators who have not learned to balance their voices.

Silliness

Silliness is regularly ignored as a showing tool and is not supported over and over in schools. Chuckling releases both education and under-studies pressure and strain.

You ought to build up the capacity to giggle at yourself and urge understudies to do likewise. It encourages a neighbourly domain that encourages learning.

Satisfactory information on the topic is significant to your prosperity; be that as it may, it's not by any means the only pivotal component.

It is making an atmosphere that encourages learning and maintenance requests great nonverbal and verbal aptitudes.

Contact

Contact is a generally utilised type of non-verbal communication device.

By contacting, one can express a wide scope of feelings. In any case, the acknowledged methods of touch shift contingent upon the sexual orientation, age, relative status, closeness, and social foundation of the persons.

For instance, with regards to our way of life, when one contacts you from the rear of the assessment lobby, you comprehend that he needs to know something.

Quiet

Quiet is an amazing asset for communication. It might have a positive or negative significance.

In a study hall, quiet show that understudies are listening cautiously and attentively. Similarly, through quietness, one can impart his absence of intrigue or an inability to comprehend.

For instance, quietness frequently shows that a person accepting guidance doesn't comprehend the activity required, or sometimes quietness demonstrates assent.

Personal Appearance

Appearance is additionally a significant non-verbal communication device. Appearance incorporates dress, hair, adornments, cosmetics, belt clasps, etc.

Appearance demonstrates the level of significance or intrigue a person passes on to an event. By methods for uniform, we can distinguish an understudy, a specialist, a legal advisor, a cop, and so on.

The dress in an association is seen to fit with recognised appearance models. Workers can wear distinctive clothing, for example, when they protest than when they work.

Image

An image is something that speaks to a thought, a physical element, or a procedure yet is particular from it. The motivation behind an image is to convey meaning.

For instance, a red octagon might be an image for "stop."

On a guide, an image of a tent may speak to a campground. Numeric images are numeric. Personal names are people's photos. A red rose is a love.

Visual Communication

At the point when communication happens by methods for any visual guides, it'sknown as visual communication.

Accordingly, communication that happens through outward appearance, personal appearance, motion, act, printed picture, sign, signal, image, map, publication, slide, chart, outline, diagram, and so on is called visual communication.

To define ' danger, ' for example, we use red sign; to show ' risky, ' we use a skull held on a cross-section between two bits of bone; to explain ' no smoking, ' we use an illustration with a cross-print showing a lighted cigarette.

Significance of Nonverbal Communication comprehending what you will say is just part of the image similarly, as significant is having a comprehension of how to pass on your messages through your body language.

Some significant focuses on communicating the significance, need, focal points, or elements of non-verbal communication are talked about beneath:

•   **Well Expression of the Speaker's Attitude**

Different non-verbal prompts of the speaker like physical developments, outward appearance, a method for articulation, and so forth assume a significant job in communicating the inward importance of the messages in up close and personal conversation and meeting.

For instance, the outward appearance of the speaker shows his frame of mind, assurance profundity of information, and so forth.

- **Providing Information Regarding the Sender of the Written Message**

The organisation, tidiness, language, and the presence of the envelope utilised in a composed message send a non-verbal message concerning the essayist's tests, decision, level of training, and so forth.

- **Expressing the Attitude of the Listener and Receiver.**

Sometimes the presence of the audience members and collectors passes on their frames of mind, sentiments, and contemplations concerning the messages they have read or heard.

- **Gaining Knowledge about a Class of People**

Garments, hairdo, tidiness, adornments, beautifying agents, and stature of people pass on impressions concerning their occupation, age, nationality, social or monetary level, work status, and so on.

For instance, understudies, cops, medical attendants, And so on can be recognised by their clothes without much of a stretch.

- ### **Gaining Knowledge about the Status of a Person**

Non-verbal signs likewise help to decide the general status of persons working in an association. For instance, room size, area, goods, designs, lightings, and so forth demonstrate the situation of a person in the association.

- ### **Communicating Common Message to All People**

Now and again, non-verbal prompts can viably express many genuine messages more precisely than those of some other technique for communication.

The use of red, yellow and green signals and other indicators for road vehicles, for example.

- ### **Communicating with the Handicapped People**

Non-verbal prompts of communication extraordinarily help in speaking with the impeded people.

For instance, the language of communication with the hard of hearing relies upon the developments of the hands, fingers, and eyeballs.

- **Conveying Message to the IlliteratePeople**

Communication with uneducated people through-composed media is unthinkable. There may likewise be a few circumstances that don't enable the utilisation of oral media to speak with them.

The media of communications in such circumstances are used by non-verbal approaches such as images, nuances, diagrams, signs, and images.

For instance, to demonstrate risk, we utilise red sign, and to mean hazardous, we utilise a skull put between two bits of bone put in an across the style.

- **Quick Expression of Message**

Non-verbal prompts like sign and image can likewise impart a few messages rapidly than composed or oral media.

For instance;If drivers of the running vehicle have to tell us that the street is tight or there is a turn on the road ahead, we use signs or images to a large extent as opposed to using a composed or oral message.

- **Presenting Information Precisely**

Sometimes quantitative data on any issue may require a long composed message. Be that as it may, this quantitative data can be exhibited effectively and exactly through tables, diagrams, charts, and so on.

NOTE:

Non-verbal communication can take numerous structures relying upon the circumstance, the capacity of communicators, and so forth. To improve your nonverbal aptitudes, record your talking on tape. At that point, ask an associate in communications to propose refinements.

STRATEGIES AND TECHNIQUES TO ANALYZE PEOPLE

The capacity to read others will significantly influence how you manage them. You can adjust your message and communication style to make sure that it is conceived in the perfect way when you see how anyone else feels.

In any case, what better would you do?

Also, what different signs can warn you to what somebody is thinking or feeling?

1. Watch Body Language Cues

Research has demonstrated that words represent just 7 percent of how we convey while our body language (55 percent) and voice tone (30 percent) speak to the rest. Here, the give up to concentrate on is relinquishing, making a decent attempt to read body language prompts. Try not to get excessively extreme or investigative. Remain loose and liquid. Be agreeable, sit back, and watch.

• **Pay Attention to Appearance When reading others notice:** Are they wearing a power suit and well-sparkled shoes, dressed for progress, demonstrating aspiration? Pants and a T-shirt, demonstrating solace with being easygoing? A tight top with cleavage, an enticing decision? A pendant, for example, across or Buddha showing profound qualities?

- **Notice Posture When reading people's stance, ask yourself:** Do they hold their head high, confident? Or then again do they walk falteringly or fall, an indication of low self-regard? Do they swagger with a puffed-out chest, an indication of a major conscience?

- Watch for Physical Movements,Leaning, and separation—Observe where people lean. For the most part, we lean toward those we like and away from those we don't.

- Crossed arms and legs—This posture recommends preventiveness, outrage, or self-insurance. As people spread their arms, they usually point the top leg to the person with whom they are quieter.

- Hiding one's hands—When people place their hands in their laps, pockets, or put them despite their good faith, it recommends that they are concealing something.

- Lip gnawing or fingernail skin picking—When people nibble or lick their lips or pick their fingernail skin, they are attempting to relieve themselves under strain or in a clumsy circumstance.

- Interpret Facial ExpressionEmotions can get carved on our countenances. Profound glare lines recommend stress or over-thinking. Smile lines of happiness are Crow's feet. The lips signal anger, hatred, or harshness. They're under pressure. Pressure indications are an influenced jaw and granulation of the teeth.

2. Tune in to Your Intuition

You can tune into somebody past their body language and words. Instinct is the thing that your gut feels, not what your head says. It's nonverbal data you see using pictures and ah-has, instead of rationale. If you need to get somebody, what tallies the most is who the person is, not their external trappings. Instinct gives you a chance to see more remote than the conspicuous to uncover a more extravagant story.

Agenda of Intuitive Cues:

- Honour your premonitions: Tune in to what your gut says, particularly during first gatherings, an instinctive response that happens before you get an opportunity to think. It transfers whether you're calm or not. Premonitions happen rapidly, a base reaction. They're your internal truth meter, handing-off on the off chance that you can confide in people.

•   Feel the goosebumps: Goosebumps are radiant instinctive shivers that pass on that we reverberate with people who move or move us or are stating something that inspires an emotional response. Goosebumps additionally happen when you experience this feels familiar, an acknowledgement that you've known somebody previously. However, you've ever met.

•   Pay thoughtfulness regarding flashes of understanding

In conversations, you may get an "ah-ha" about people who arrive instantly. Remain alert. Else, you may miss it. We will work in general go onto the following idea so quickly these basic bits of knowledge are lost.

•   Watch for natural compassion: Sometimes, you can feel people's physical indications and feelings in your body, which is an extreme type of sympathy.

Things being what they are, when reading people, notice: "Does my back harmed when it didn't previously?

Am I discouraged or upset after an uneventful gathering?"

To decide whether this is compassion, get input.

3. Sense Emotional Energy

Feelings are a dazzling articulation of our energy, the "vibe" we emit. We register these with instinct. A few people feel great to associate with; they improve your disposition and imperativeness. Others are depleting; you instinctually need to escape. The body pulse or feet can feel this "unexpected energy."

However, it's undetectable. In Chinese prescription, it's called chi, an essentialness that is basic to wellbeing.

Techniques to Read Emotional Energy:

•   People's Presence: This is the general energy we discharge, not consistent with words or behavior. It's the emotional climate encompassing us like a downpour cloud or the sun. As you read, people notice: Do they have a cordial nearness that pulls in you? Or, on the other hand, would you say you are getting the creeps, making you back off?

- **Watch People's Eyes**

Our eyes transmit ground-breaking energy. Similarly, as the mind has an electromagnetic sign stretching out past the body, it considers demonstrating that the eyes venture this as well. Set aside some effort to watch people's eyes. Is it true that they are minding? Hot? Serene? Mean? Furious? Likewise, decide: Is there somebody at home in their eyes, demonstrating a limit with regards to closeness? Or then again, do they appear to be watched or covering up?

- **Notice the Feel of a Handshake, Hug, and Touch**

We share emotional energy through physical contact, a lot of like an electrical flow. Ask, do you have warm, good, confident feelings with a handshake or embrace? Or it's off-pressing again, so you have to pull back? The hands of people are damp, and tension is flagging. Or then again limp, proposing being hesitant and meek?

- **Listen for Tone of Voice and Laugh:** The tone and volume of our voice can educate much concerning our feelings. Sound frequencies make vibrations. When reading people, notice how their manner of speaking influences you. Ask yourself: Does their tone feel relieving? Or, on the other hand, is it grating, short, or whiny?

Instructions to break down somebody's personality

How might you dissect somebody's personality? Is there some recipe that can assist you with getting people?

A few people say you can comprehend somebody's personality dependent on his body language,facial includes, or even how he strolls.

While this is 100% genuine as yet dissecting, somebody's personality requires further information about numerous different things other than the ones referenced.

That is the reason I chose to reveal to you how to examine somebody's personality utilising a pragmatic model that I will outline in this segment.

Pragmatic model for investigating somebody's personality

The first time I met (X), not a genuine name without a doubt, was in the rec centre. We never talked, however, I saw that the person goes to the rec centre every day at the equivalent specific time. A significant irrelevant detail for some people, yet for somebody who knows beyond what minimal about breaking down personalities, this detail can show a great deal.

The person was self-motivated, not a slacker, solid willed, mentally composed, and had a feeling of time criticalness. These traits got unmistakable to me since I saw his promptness.

One other thing was truly recognisable about that person, he used to wear garments that uncovered his muscles, and he additionally used to do odd activities that nobody does. The person was undoubtedly flashy and overlooked. I found him to be a single kid when I collected additional data.

While breaking down somebody's personality, it's critical to take note of how birth requests influence personality. Just youngsters are normally showered with consideration when they are youthful, and that is the reason they grow up attempting to stay in the focal point of consideration any place they go.

The person wanted to don dark. He wore dark all the time,even though he used to put on something else frequently. I likewise held up until he got out his portable out of his pocket and found what I was expecting, his cell phone alongside the spread were dark as well.

While examining somebody's personality, you should comprehend that people go to one outrageous when they are attempting to escape from something. Going to the exercise centre and wearing dark uncovered that the person needed to seem intense, abhorrent,and perilous. (a terrible kid).

At the point when I gathered additional data, I found what I was expecting by and by. At the point when the person was a little kid, he used to be harassed by different children, and that is the reason he felt frail. At the point when he grew up, he put forth a valiant effort to conceal his past by seeming solid. Heading off to the rec centre and wearing dark were two activities that helped him escape from quite a while ago.

Another factor you should place at the top of the priority list while examining somebody's personality is that drawing an obvious conclusion ought to consistently prompt a straight line. It means that, in the absence of chance, my intuition is correct (that that guy must be groundbreaking) at this stage that we must assume that he does different things that can motivate him to be incredibly different from those he does at the moment.

My speculation was valid. Martial arts extremely inspired by the person. Generally, a person gets inspired by what can assist him with moving towards a significant objective and away from a character that he despises (being frail for this situation)

Questions That Reveals Personality

Meeting new people is probably the best thing throughout everyday life. Each noteworthy other, companion, chief, associate, neighbour or colleague you have was once only an outsider. Furthermore, when you initially met that odder couldn't have had any thought that you'd structure the relationship you as of now appreciate - or would you be able to have?

It's difficult to learn all that you have to think about somebody the first time you meet except if you have a type of clairvoyant understanding. In any case, there are a few inquiries you can pose to that will give you a more profound, more exact image of somebody than others.

Unquestionably, straightforward inquiries, as "Are you new here?" during a systems administration occasion, or, "For what reason did you leave your last employment?" at a prospective employee meet-up will probably give you some important data. They are not enough; however, they don't tell you about the person with which you speak. They are insufficient.

As a clear difference, the accompanying inquiries. You do not only want to provide you with clearer information concerning your outsider or colleague, but also recommend the significant experience of the personalities of these people in general:

1. How might you portray yourself?

From the outset, this inquiry may appear cheating. The objective is to get a person to uncover his/her personality through optional methods, so isn't posing this inquiry a sort of alternate route?

Indeed, yes and no - it's about the uncertain expressing, "How might you portray yourself?" as opposed to, "What's your personality like?" or, "What do a great many people consider you?" Notice that there's no sign here. You're not requesting that a person depict himself/herself physically, expertly, emotionally, or in some other explicit way.

Rather, focus on the credits your interviewee decides to use to uncover first, and how outrageous their pledge decisions appear to be. Modest or compliant people will, in general, pick humbler words like "attentive" or "recreational," while rich or outgoing people pick all the more dominant words like "smart" or "athletic."

2. What is your greatest achievement?

This one gives you one basic bit of understanding into a person's past, yet additionally reveals to both of you unpretentious things about their personality. In the first place, it shows where this current individual's greatest advantages lie; once more, the inquiry is questionable does as well, the person reacts with an expert achievement or a personal one?

Additionally, to what extent prior did this achievement occur? How can he/she act in bringing it up? Next, to what extent did it take to consider it? On the off chance that this "achievement" comes simply after a long delay, that could be an indication of either numerous or not many past achievements. You'll need to test further to discover.

3. Have you read any great books recently?

The appropriate responses you'll arrive change uncontrollably. To begin with, note the contrast among readers and non-readers. You'll get the incidental person who'll concede, "I don't read books," yet more frequently, among non-readers, you'll discover people delaying quite a while before thinking of a book, or returning to a great secondary school or school content.

Among genuine readers, you'll find prominent novel shoppers, business and self-help readers, writing fans, pop science followers, and a few different types.

4. What is your fantasy work?

The more equivocal the inquiry, the better it is. The inquiry isn't, "What do you need in your next activity?" or, "Where do you see yourself in five years?" at the same time, "What is your fantasy work?" A sycophant can depict the activity of the individual in question at a prospective employee meeting.Others may feature innovative interests. Still, others will portray employments that don't exist (or are incredibly uncommon), like "brew tester" or "young doggie cuddler."

Whatever the reaction, it will reveal to you whether somebody's given this a great deal of thought or has never considered it.

5. Who is your saint?

This inquiry gets you data that is somewhat more explicit and increasingly wise - through an undeniable course. Be that as it may, I've thought that it was a significant inquiry to pose. You'll discover people who depict a relative or somebody they knew throughout everyday life; people who respect a competitor or mainstream society big name; and people who turn upward to effective business people or businesspeople.

You may have the option to perceive something about the insight or age of the person you're talking to here, yet more critically, you'll learn about their qualities. Would it be that makes this "saint" stand apart above any other individual who, at any point, lived?

Generally, a portion of these inquiries are excessively forward to ask arbitrary outsiders in the city; however, once you've heated another contact, don't hesitate to break these out. How such people respond, how they answer, and how they state their answers will say a lot about the type of person remaining before you.

NEGATIVE BODY LANGUAGE: EXAMPLES AND SIGNS

In this exercise, you'll learn the meaning of negative body language and what its various structures can mean. The exercise will likewise address the social contrasts in body language.

Negative Body Language

Body language can inform a great deal regarding how a person feels. A drooped stance can exhibit an absence of certainty or fatigue. Turned away, eye to eye connection can be a pointer that a person is awkward, self-cognizant, or in any event, lying. Crossed arms can flag preventiveness or contradiction. A constrained smile can mean deviousness. How astonishing is it that the body can impart such a significant number of things without the person talking a word?

Negative body language is either a cognizant or an oblivious articulation of negative sentiments through developments of the body. Being gifted at seeing contrary body language can help one with personal or expert connections and knowing when another is disappointed or despondent. It can recognise what negative body language to maintain a strategic distance from if one needs to leave a decent impression on a group of people or audience. Body language can be significantly more significant than verbally expressed words.

Types of Negative Body Language

We should investigate a portion of the various types of negative body language and what they might be conveying:

1. Shirking of eye to eye connection

Apprehension, absence of certainty, low self-regard, or untrustworthiness.

If a person doesn't look, they may feel uncomfortable. This discomfort can be attributed to low self-consciousness, certainty, or lying fears. Researchers have broadly looked into how to pinpoint lying through eye to eye connection, and their discoveries have been uncertain. It appears that a few people look to one side when lying, and others give conscious and constrained eye to eye connection when lying. It's difficult to tell.

2. Gazing: power and excitement

Giving a lot of eye to eye connection, then again, can make one look excessively enthusiastic and lead to an unbalanced trade. The beneficiary of the eye to eye connection will most likely feel uneasy.

3. Crossed arms: separateness, distress, or preventiveness

On the off chance that you watch people talking at a party, you will locate that many remain with their arms or submits in front of them. You can cross your arms, or your hands can be fastened before your groin.It could be an unavoidable impediment to each other and the person with whom they speak. Talking to one's side with arms can then again show transparency and neighbourliness.

4. Abuse of hands: apprehension, energy, or madness

These signs can be seen in a person who speaks quickly, while his hands fly all over. He can be a sign that a person is apprehensive or hypersensitive.

5. Seeing watch, clock or phone: weariness, uneasiness, eagerness, or future-disapproved

At the point when people are taking a gander at a phone, watch, or clock during a conversation, it is typically an indication that they are in a rush for it to be complete. They might be blocking out the other person and contemplating what they need to do straightaway.

6. Poor stance: the absence of certainty, reluctance, absence of capacity, inaccessibility, or fatigue

Poor attitudes can prove that someone is not trustworthy or self-assured. Balanced persons are received more respectfully and are seen in the United States as being ever more educated and sound.

7. Glaring: bitterness, compassion, discontent, or outrage

Scowling is an undeniable pointer of these feelings. If a speaker is recounting to a miserable story, a glaring audience may simply be relating. In any case, if the speaker isn't recounting to a pitiful story, the audience might be troubled, irate, or dismal. A wrinkle between the eyes or a snugness of the face can mean something very similar.

8. Perspiring: anxiety

Poor attitudes can prove that somebody isn't confident or confident. Balanced individuals are received more respectfully and are viewed more and more educated and sound in the United States.

9. Hands behind back: doubtful or secretive

In the United States, hands behind the back may imply that a person is attempting to shroud something. It is frightening for some not to have the option to see the other person's hands while speaking with them.

10. Grasped clench hands: outrage or forcefulness

Grasped hands, as a rule,e, demonstrate that a person is ready to battle or that they are furious and may get forceful if further incited.

POSITIVE BODY LANGUAGE: EXAMPLES AND SIGNS

In this exercise, we will learn about ways to deal with positive body language, for example, standing up tall, handshakes, and grinning. We will likewise consider the manners by which we move our bodies that don't flag energy, and ways we can improve those things.

What is Body Language?

The developments and places of our bodies which express our musings or sentiments are what makeup body language. For instance, have you at any point remained with your arms crossed, tapping your foot? What may that mean? Is it accurate to say that you are exhausted, or possibly anxious? What about on the off chance that you have a smile all over and hold your hand out to present yourself? It may mean that you are happy to meet the person you welcome warmly; this is the positive language of the body. In this workout, we will examine a few cases of positive body language, just like we will examine what these signals mean.

Occupied Feet

One approach to know how somebody truly feels about the circumstance they are in is to watch their feet. People who need certainty or are apprehensive will rearrange or somewhat kick their feet. They may likewise squirm with their feet or wind them around furniture. This is done intuitively regularly. In other words, we don't realise we're doing it. You can learn to reduce these signals by focusing on the development of your body. Remember this when you're in trouble or meet someone just because of it. Or, on the other hand, come to someone else to watch and raise you. You will be shocked to find out that you had no knowledge of your feet in such a way!

Approaches to Portray Yourself Positively

Have you, at any point, been on a meeting for work you truly needed? You already have the entirety of the capabilities and the correct tutoring. All in all, what else would you be able to do to establish an incredible first connection? Utilise your body language. That is the thing that! While presenting yourself, stand up tall. By doing this, you depict power and achievement. At the point when you have a great stance, you additionally appear as though you believe in yourself. Consider it. On the off chance that you see somebody slouched over and taking a gander at the ground, do they seem as though they feel confident? Likely not. The following thing you ought to do is keep in touch.

It maybe cumbersome and troublesome if you are thoughtful or modest. However, like this, the people around you will realise that you are keen on them. This additional motion toward people that you are focusing on what they are stating. Moreover, when somebody asks you an inquiry, talk with your hands, and utilise open motions. By demonstrating the palms of your hands while talking, you intuitively advise people that you don't have anything to cover up, which signals validity. At last, by utilising a solid handshake and a smile, you make a bond and leave an enduring positive impression.

Low-Effort versus High-Effort Thinking: Advantages and Disadvantages

Our intellectual wheels are consistently moving, regardless of whether we don't understand it. In this exercise, we examine thinking and separate between low-exertion and high-exertion thinking. We likewise talk about the focal points and burdens of each type of reasoning.

Thinking

The greater part of us don't ponder thinking; we take care of business. However, we think throughout the day. We decide, recall certainties, apply information, etc. We think in any event when we don't understand it, as our mind forms the data we take inconsistently. Analysts separate considerations into a wide range of classifications. But all kinds of thinking can be sorted by low effort or high effort thinking. How do we deal with every type of argument and each one's preferences and disadvantages?

Low-Effort Thinking

One type or classification of reasoning is low-exertion thinking, which is imagining that is programmed and automatic. It is a social perception that requires almost no to no exertion. When strolling into life with twelve people, you can without much of a stretch differentiate between a conference and a frock party. You don't need to remain at the entryway and cautiously watch everything about recognise what's happening. Each programmed judgment we make, for example, this one, without intentionally thinking about other options, includes low-exertion thinking.

At the point when we play out an errand on autopilot, we likewise occupied with low-exertion thinking. At the point when we ride a bicycle, for instance, we don't ordinarily consider every development it takes to remain on the bicycle and keep it pushing ahead. At the point when we're driving, and the stoplight turns red, we hammer on the brakes regularly without intentionally choosing to do as such.

Low-Effort Thinking: Advantages and Disadvantages

There are positive focal points to low-exertion thinking. For one, it spares us a lot of time and exertion, so we don't need to spend the whole day contemplating all that we experience. Low-exertion thinking can happen out of sight of our brains while we effectively consider or potentially accomplish something different. Have you, at any point, been driving on a street you've driven many times and scattered while pondering your day? Even though you may have been effectively considering that conversation you had before, you were as yet ready to utilise low-exertion thinking to guide, keep up your speed, and so forth.

More often than not, low-exertion suspecting serves us well and encourages us to size up another circumstance or data rapidly and precisely. Be that as it may, because we don't control low-exertion figuring, it can push us into difficulty. For example, it can lead us to make fake suspicions or even to control a racial tendency we do not understand.

High-Effort Thinking

Even though a lot of everyday life requires minimal psychological exertion, different things take significantly more ideas. For instance, a great many people cautiously think about which school to visit, what to wear to their wedding, or which vehicle to purchase. These choices include high-exertion thinking - imagining that is controlled and purposeful. That's a social insight that takes lots of effort. You are aware that you think when you're busy with high-effort thinking.

At the point when we learn something new, we need to consider the bit by bit process that we perform deliberately. At the point when we previously learned how to ride a bicycle, for instance, the procedure appeared to be entangled. We were deliberately controlled at the time and were so occupied with a strong sense of the exercise. The procedure was programmed over the long term, and we can now play the job with little effort and effectiveness.

Positive Body Language - Importance

Body language is of the most extreme significance in this exceptionally aggressive world. The corporate segment esteems great body language a ton, and any indication of awful body language can break bargains in any event, prompting the loss of system for people.

A familiar proverb says, "Activities talk stronger than words." Our body act, alongside its developments and situation of various body parts, assume a significant job in letting out our sentiments and feelings, regardless of whether we don't show the feelings intentionally.

Self-assured Behavior

A positive body language causes the person to be increasingly confident and helps with putting their assessment forward more effectively than the others. Others enjoy positive body language, and henceforth, the person conveying a positive body language gets more consideration and support in any exchange.

Non-verbal Communication

Research says that our communication comprises of 35% verbal communication and 65% non-verbal communication. It infers whatever we talk intentionally involves only 35% of what the other person makes out of us. Our body language teaches 65 per cent of data about us. Our body language helps other people distinguish our feelings, status, and even our way of life.

Non-verbal communication assumes a critical job related to the expressed words. Our non-verbal communication can emphasise our message, repudiate our words, fortify our announcement, substitute the importance of our sentences, and supplement the significance of our words. Since non-verbal communication can either stress our point or negate it, it is important to keep our body language in a state of harmony with our feelings. Any indication of contention between the body language and our words can cause us to seem conniving and misleading.

Work environment Success

Positive body language is an unquestionable requirement in working environments and a professional workplace. Sound body language can assist in cultivating with joining the soul in the work environment, which can likewise support the spirit of the representatives. The designation of duties gets simpler through positive body language. It can likewise help in passing on regard for associates and settling clashes in the association.

During corporate gatherings, one can show intrigue, gathering, and bliss utilising positive body language. A delicate smile, open palms, inclining forward, and eye to eye connection can go far in setting up compatibility with someone else in the gathering, accordingly helping manufacture and support a sound association with different parties in a gathering.

Connections

Negative body language can offer

Path to a great deal of distortion and mistaken assumptions. Keeping up a body stance and crazy body developments that is hostile to the next person can demolish a relationship.

For example, you have to comprehend the feelings and mindset of the other person and need to alter your behavior likewise. On the off chance that your companion is feeling great, at that point, it is alright to snicker or prod her at times. In any case, a similar movement can be misconstrued as mockery or touchy behavior if the life partner isn't feeling great. It can prompt issues among couples and can likewise prompt harmed connections.

Open Speaking

Openly, body language accepts an out and out of the various signs. If the speaker has a protective body language or has a detached body language, there are high possibilities that the individual in question won't be tuned in to eagerly by the group of spectators.

The effect factor of such talks additionally is diminished by a huge part as the group of spectators gets 35% of the whole communication yet misses the staying 65%. Henceforth, it's profoundly imperative to have appropriate body developments and stance while talking in front of an audience before a group of people.

Body language is significant in all types of communication. It breaks the boundary of newness and structures a superior associate with the beneficiary of data.

Great Standing Postures

The greater part of the times when we meet people, we are remaining before them. Be it an easygoing gathering on the roadside or meeting somebody in the workplace or having a conversation with a companion at a party, a considerable lot of the conversations throughout our life occurs in a standing position.

The following are the significant stances to search for while standing and having a conversation.

Rule 1: Stand Erect

The main point to be remembered is to remain with the spine erect. The back must be straight, as this gives an impression of being tall. A taller appearance makes a great impression too. You should not slump or hunch.

Slouching or slumping gives an impression of apathy and torpidity. A person won't prefer to move toward you to talk if you give off an impression of being frail or torpid. People constantly favour dynamic personalities. Awful standing stance likewise symbolises low self-regard. It is not a decent credit to wear while standing.

Rule 2: Face the Person

The subsequent point to recollect is to not confront sideways from your audience. Try to face up to the person with whom you speak.Standing sideways shows that you need to flee from the person and would prefer not to keep talking. Watch out for an indistinguishable sign from the other person from well. On the off chance that that person is standing sideways if it's not too much trouble stopping the conversation at the earliest opportunity. It is because the other person isn't keen on the conversation.

The ideal approach to stand is to coordinate your heart towards the other person. Guarantee that your heart faces the heart of the other person with no block in the middle. Remaining with arms traversed the chest is additionally a major 'No.' It is smarter to stand akimbo or with your hands over your midriff. Having crossed arms symbolisesa cautious position or self observer nature. People only here and there prefer it type of demeanour, and it puts a large portion of the people off.

Rule 3: Free Your Hands

The third point to be cautious about is not to put your hands inside your pockets while talking to somebody. This stance shows disregard. Keeping hands in the pocket shows that a person isn't intrigued to talk. Recall that arms are the vocal harmonies of body language and can say a lot about your frame of mind and intrigue.

Rule 4: Look into the Eyes

The fourth point to be cautious about is to investigate the eyes of the other person without scaring that person. If you get looking far from the other person, it will show an absence of enthusiasm for the conversation on your part. Continue searching for these signs in the other person as well. Maybe, the other person is turning away from you for more often than not. That will imply that the person isn't engaged in you, and consequently, it is smarter to release the person.

Rule 5: Move, Yet Mind Your Limbs

Last yet not least, it is alright to have some appendage developments. Moving hands to a limited degree show your enthusiasm for the conversation and your energy levels as well. Try not to fuss a lot with hands, and attempt to keep your palms open. You ought to likewise remain with your legs apart. Remember not to play with your nose using your hands because that symbolises timidity and lack of certainty. Crossed legs imply vulnerability and shut nature.

SIMPLE UNDERSTAND BODY LANGUAGE

Understanding Body Language

Body language alludes to the nonverbal sign that we use to impart. As indicated by specialists, these nonverbal signs make up a gigantic part of day by day communication. From our outward appearances to our body developments, the things we don't state can, in any case, pass on volumes of data.

Regardless of whether at the workplace or out with companions, the body language of the people around you says a lot. It suggested that the language of the body should establish more than 60 percent of what we give. Thus it is important to learn to read nonverbal signals.

From eye behavior to the bearing in which a person focuses their feet, body language uncovers what a person is truly thinking.

The following are important hints to help you learn how to read and understand body language better.

CONCENTRATE THE EYES

Eyes Body LanguageEyebehavior can be extremely telling. When speaking with somebody, focus on whether the individual looks or turns away. Failure to look can demonstrate weariness, lack of engagement, or even double-dealing – particularly when somebody turns away and to the side. On the off chance that a person looks down, then again, it frequently shows apprehension or accommodation. Additionally, check for widened understudies to decide whether somebody is reacting well toward you.

Understudies enlarge when psychological exertion increments, so on the off chance that somebody centred around a person or thing they like, their students will consequently widen. Student widening can be hard to recognise. However, under the correct conditions, you ought to have the option to spot it. A person's squinting rate can likewise say a lot about what is happening internally — rate increases when people think more or focus more. Increased flickering rates are now and then lying – especially when connected to your face (especially your mouth and eyes).

Looking at something can propose a longing for that thing. For instance, if somebody looks at the entryway, this may demonstrate a craving to leave. Looking at a person can demonstrate a craving to talk to that person. With regards to eye behavior, it likewise proposed that looking upwards and to one side during conversation demonstrates an untruth has been said while looking upwards and to one side shows the person is coming clean.

The purpose behind this is people turn upward and to one side when utilising their creative mind to compose a story, and gaze upward and to one side when they are reviewing a genuine memory.

LOOK AT THE FACE – BODY LANGUAGE TOUCHING MOUTH OR SMILING

Even though people are bound to control their outward appearance, you can even now get on significant nonverbal prompts on the off chance that you give close consideration. Give particular consideration to the mouth when attempting to translate nonverbal behavior. A great signal can be a basic fascination method in smile body language. Grinning is an important nonverbal search engine. There are different smiles, such as certified smiles and telephone smiles.

A certifiable smile draws in the entire face, while a phoney smile uses the mouth. A veritable smile proposes that the person is upbeat and appreciate the organisation of the people around the person in question. A phoney smile, then again, is intended to pass on joy or endorsement; however,it recommends that the smiler is feeling something different. A "half-smile" is another regular facial behavior that draws in a single side of the mouth and demonstrates mockery or vulnerability.

You may likewise see a slight frown that endures not exactly a second before somebody smiles. It ordinarily proposes the person is concealing their disappointment behind a phoney smile. Tight, tightened lips additionally demonstrate disappointment, while a casual mouth shows a casual demeanour and positive state of mind. Covering the mouth or contacting the lips with the hands or fingers when talking might be a marker of lying.

FOCUS ON PROXIMITY

Closeness is the separation between you and the other person. Focus on how close somebody stands or sits alongside you to decide whether they see you well. Standing or sitting in nearness to somebody is maybe probably the best marker of affinity. Then again, on the off chance that somebody backs up or moves away when you move in nearer, this could be an indication that the association isn't shared.

You can inform a great deal regarding the type of relationship two people have simply by watching the nearness between them. Remember that a few societies incline toward less or more separation during collaboration, so closeness isn't constantly an exact marker of fondness with somebody.

CHECK WHETHER THE OTHER PERSON IS MIRRORING YOU

Reflecting includes emulating the other person's body language. While collaborating with somebody, verify whether the person reflects your behavior. For instance, if you are sitting at a table with somebody and lay an elbow on the table, hold up 10 seconds to check whether the other person does likewise.

Another normal reflecting signal includes tasting a beverage simultaneously. If somebody imitates your body language, this is a generally excellent sign that the individual in question is attempting to set up an affinity with you. Have a go at changing your body stance and check whether the other person changes their correspondingly.

WATCH THE HEAD MOVEMENT

If you talk, a person shows comprehension – or lack of – the pace at which they are behaving. Slow gesturing shows that the person is keen on what you are stating and needs you to keep talking. Quick gesturing demonstrates the person has sufficiently heard and needs you to get done with talking or give that person ago to talk. Tilting the head sideways during conversation can be an indication of enthusiasm for what the other person is stating.

Tilting the head in reverse can be an indication of doubt or vulnerability. People also point to people they want or have partiality with their heads or faces. In gatherings and gatherings, you can tell who the people with control depend on how regularly people take a gander at them. Then again, the less-noteworthy people are taken a gander at less frequently.

TAKE A GANDER AT THE OTHER PERSON'S FEET

Eyes Body LanguageA part of the body where people regularly "release" significant nonverbal prompts is the feet. The reason why people impart nonverbal messages unpredictably is that they usually focus on controlling their external appearance and positioning the chest area so that important information can be garnered with their feet. When standing or sitting, a person will, for the most part, point their feet toward the path they need to go.

So if you notice that someone's feet are directed to you, it can be a decent sign that you are well assessed. It applies to one-on-one connection and gathering cooperation. You can enlighten a great deal concerning bunch elements just by contemplating the body language of people included, particularly what direction their feet are pointing.

Also, on the off chance that somebody gives off an impression of being occupied with a conversation with you. Yet, their feet are pointing toward another person. It's presumably the individual in question would prefer to talk to that person (in any case if the chest area prompts propose something else).

WATCH FOR HAND SIGNALS

Hands Body Language Like the feet, the hands release significant nonverbal prompts when looking a body language. It is a significant hint when reading body language, so give close consideration to this next part. Watch body language submits pockets when standing. Search for particular hand signals, for example, the other person placing their hands in their pockets or hand on head. It can show anything from anxiety to inside and out double-dealing. Oblivious pointing showed by hand signals can likewise say a lot.

When making hand motions, a person will point in the general course of the person they share a fondness with (this nonverbal prompt is particularly essential to watch for during gatherings and while connecting in gatherings). Supporting the head with the hand by laying an elbow on the table can show that the person is listening and is keeping the head still to centre. Supporting the head with the two elbows on the table, then again, can demonstrate fatigue.

The hindrance that is meant to shut the other person off, at the point when a person contains an item entre the person with whom he is associated. For instance, in nonverbal communication, if two people speak, and one person keeps a stack of paper before that person, this is considered a blocking demonstration.

ANALYSE THE POSITION OF THE ARMS

Hands Body LanguageThink of a person's arms as the entryway to the body and the self. On the off chance that a person folds their arms while collaborating with you, it is generally observed as a cautious, blocking motion. Crossed arms can likewise show nervousness, powerlessness, or a shut personality.

Whenever crossed arms are joined by a certified smile and by and large loosened up pose, at that point, it can demonstrate a confident, loosened up frame of mind. At the point when somebody puts their hands on their hips, it is normally used to apply predominance and is utilised by men more frequently than ladies.

BODY AND FACIAL EXPRESSIONS

The body language could represent from 60 to 65% of all communication.

Understanding body language is significant. However, it is additionally fundamental to focus on different prompts, for example, setting. Much of the time, you should take a gander at signals as a gathering as opposed to concentrating on a solitary activity.

Here is What To Look For When You're Trying To Interpret Body Language.

Outward appearances

Ponder how much a person can pass on with only an outward appearance. A smile can show endorsement or bliss. A glare can flag dissatisfaction or misery. Now and again, our outward appearances may uncover our actual emotions about a particular circumstance. While you state that you are feeling fine, the expression all over may tell people generally.

Only a few examples of emotions can be expressed in the face

- Happiness

- Sadness

- Anger

- Surprise

- Disgust

- Fear

- Confusion

- Excitement

- Desire

- Contempt

The appearance on a person's face can even help decide whether we trust or accept what the individual is stating. One examination found that the most dependable outward appearance included a slight cause of a commotion and a slight smile. This articulation, the scientists recommended, passes on both cordiality and certainty.

Outward appearances are additionally among the most all-inclusive types of body language. The expressions used to pass on dread, outrage, misery, and joy are comparable all through the world.

Scientist Paul Ekman has discovered help for all-inclusiveness of an assortment of outward appearances attached to particular feelings, including bliss, outrage, dread, shock, and pity.

Research even proposes that we make decisions about people's knowledge, dependent on their appearances and expressions. One study showed that persons with smaller faces and increasingly visible nose were keenly perceived. Besides, people with a smiling and cheerful articulation decided to be wiser than people with wrathful expressions.

The Eyes

The eyes are now and again alluded to as the "windows to the spirit" since they are fit for uncovering a lot about what a person is feeling or thinking. As you participate in a conversation with someone else, observing eye developments is a characteristic and significant part of the communication procedure. Some normal things you may see incorporate whether people are looking or deflecting their look, the amount they are squinting, or if their students are enlarged.

When Evaluating Body Language, Pay Attention To The Following Eye Signals:

Eye stare:

At the point when a person looks legitimately at you while having a conversation, it demonstrates that they are intrigued and focusing. Be that as it may, delayed eye to eye connection can feel compromising. Then again, looking away and regularly turning away may demonstrate that the person is diverted, awkward, or attempting to cover their genuine emotions.

Squinting:

Squinting is characteristic, yet you ought to likewise focus on whether a person is flickering excessively or excessively little. People regularly flicker all the more quickly when they are feeling upset or awkward. Rare flickering may show that a person is purposefully attempting to control their eye movements.7 For instance, a poker player may squint less much of the time since he is intentionally attempting to seem unexcited about the hand he manages.

Student size:

Student size can be an unobtrusive nonverbal communication signal. While light levels in the earth control understudy widening, sometimes feelings can likewise cause small changes in student size. For instance, you may have heard the expression "room eyes" used to depict the look somebody gives when they pull in to someone else. Exceptionally widened eyes, for instance, can show that a person is intrigued or even excited.

THE MOUTH

Mouth expressions and developments can likewise be basic in reading body language. For instance, biting on the base lip may show that the individual is encountering sentiments of stress, dread, or weakness.

Covering the mouth might be a push to be amiable if the person is yawning or hacking, yet it might likewise be an endeavour to conceal a scowl of objection. Grinning is maybe one of the best body language signals. However,Multiple points of view can also Determine yourself by smiles. A smile might be certifiable, or it might be utilised to express bogus satisfaction, mockery, or even negativity.

When Evaluating Body Language, Pay Attention To The Following Mouth And Lip Signals:

Pressed together lips: Tightening the lips may be a marker of abhorrence, dissatisfaction, or doubt.

Lip gnawing: People sometimes chomp their lips when they are concerned, restless, or pushed.

Covering the mouth: When people need to shroud an emotional response, they may cover their mouths to abstain from showing smiles or grins.

Turned up or down: Slight changes in the mouth can likewise be unobtrusive pointers of what a person is feeling. When the mouth is slightly up, it may imply that the person is feeling cheerful or hopeful. Then again, a somewhat down-turned mouth can be a marker of misery, dissatisfaction, or even an out and out scowl.

Motions

Motions can be probably the most immediate and evident body language signals. Waving, indicating, and utilising the fingers to show numerical sums are,for the most part, normal and straightforward signals. A few motions might be social, be that as it may, so offering a go-ahead or a gesture of goodwill in another nation may have unexpected importance in comparison to it does in the United States.

The Following Examples Are Just A Few Common Gestures And Their Possible Meanings:

•	A held clench hand can show outrage in certain circumstances or solidarity in others.

- Approval and disapproval are regularly utilised as signals of endorsement and dissatisfaction.

- The "alright" motion, made by contacting together the thumb and pointer around while broadening the other three fingers,may be used to signify "alright" or "all right."10 In certain parts of Europe, be that as it may, a similar sign is utilised to infer you are nothing. In some South American nations, the image is a profane motion.

- The V sign, made by lifting the list and centre finger and isolating them to make a V-shape, implies harmony or triumph in certain nations. In the United Kingdom and Australia, the image takes on hostile importance when the rear of the hand is confronting outward.

THE ARMS AND LEGS

The arms and legs can likewise help pass on nonverbal data. Intersection the arms can demonstrate protectiveness. Intersection legs from someone else may show abhorrence or inconvenience with that individual.

Another unobtrusive flag, for example, Broadly extending your arms could be an effort to seem larger or more instructing, while maintaining your arm close to your body could serve as a way to limit or reverse your consideration.

At the point when You Are Evaluating Body Language, Pay Attention To Some Of The Following Signals That The Arms And Legs May Convey:

- Crossed arms may demonstrate that a person feels guarded, self-defensive, or cut off.

- Standing with hands set on the hips can be a sign that a person is ready and in charge, or it can likewise be an indication of forcefulness.

- Clasping the hands behind the back may show that a person is feeling exhausted, on edge, or even irate.

- Rapidly tapping fingers or squirming can be an indication that a person is exhausted, anxious, or disappointed.

- Crossed legs can demonstrate that a person is feeling shut off or needing security.

Stance

How we hold our bodies can likewise fill in as a significant part of body language. The term pose alludes to how we hold our bodies just as the general physical type of an individual. Stance can pass on an abundance of data about how a person is feeling just as insights about personality qualities, for example, regardless of whether a person is confident, open, or compliant.

Sitting upright, for instance, may show that a person is engaged and focusing on what's happening. Sitting with the body slouched forward, then again, can suggest that the person is exhausted or impassive.

When you try to read the language of the body, try and see a portion of the sign a person could send.

- Open pose includes keeping the storage compartment of the body open and uncovered. This type of stance shows agreeableness, receptiveness, and eagerness.

- The closing act includes concealing the storage compartment of the body frequently by slouching forward and keeping the arms and legs crossed. This type of stance can be a pointer of antagonistic vibe, threat, and uneasiness.

PERSONAL SPACE

Have you, at any point, heard somebody allude to their requirement for personal space? Have you at any point started to feel awkward when somebody stands only excessively near you?

The term proxemics, begat by anthropologist Edward T. Corridor, alludes to the separation between people as they communicate. Similarly, as body developments and outward appearances can impart a lot of nonverbal data, so can this physical space between individuals.

Lobby Described Four Levels Of Social Distance That Occur In Different Situations:

- **Intimate separation—6 to 18 inches:** This degree of physical separation frequently shows a closer relationship or more prominent solace between individuals. It normally happens during close contact, for example, embracing, murmuring, or contacting.

- **Personal separation—1.5 to 4 feet:** Physical separation at this level, for the most part, happens between people who are relatives or dear companions. The closer the people can serenely stand while communicating can be a pointer of the degree of closeness in their relationship.

- **Social separation—4 to 12 feet:** This degree of physical separation is regularly utilised with individuals who are colleagues. With somebody you know genuinely well, for example, a collaborator you see a few times every week, you may feel increasingly good interfacing at a closer separation. In situations where you don't have the foggiest idea about the other person well, for example, a postal conveyance driver you observe once every month, a separation of 10 to 12 feet may feel progressively good.

- **Public separation—12 to 25 feet:** Physical separation at this level is frequently utilised out in the open talking circumstances. Talking before a class brimming with understudies or giving an introduction at work are genuine instances of such circumstances.

It is likewise imperative to take note that the degree of personal separation that individuals need to feel great can change from culture to culture. One oft-referred to model is the contrast between people from Latin societies and those from North America.

People from Latin nations will, in general, feel progressively great standing more like each other as they interface while those from North America need increasingly personal separation.

A Word From Verywell

Understanding body language can go far toward helping you better speak with others and translating what others may be attempting to pass on.

While it might be enticing to dismantle flag individually, it's critical to take a gander at thisnonverbal flag in connection to verbal communication, other nonverbal sign, and the circumstance. You can likewise concentrate on learning increasingly about how to improve your nonverbal communication to turn out to be better at telling people what you are feeling—without saying a word.

CPSIA information can be obtained
at www.ICGtesting.com
Printed in the USA
LVHW051739120221
679115LV00006B/369